MICHIGAN ENGLISH TEST LISTENING & SPEAKING

STUDY GUIDE

MET TEST IDIOMS, EXERCISES, AND

PRACTICE TESTS

Michigan English Test Listening and Speaking Study Guide: MET Test Idioms, Exercises, and Practice Tests

ISBN-13: 978-1-949282-30-6

NOTE: Michigan English Test and MET are trademarks of Michigan Language Assessment in conjunction with Cambridge Assessment English, which are neither affiliated with nor endorse this publication and its related websites.

TABLE OF CONTENTS

PART 4 – MET SPEAKING PRACTICE TESTS WITH RESPONSES

Speaking Test 1 with Responses, Analysis, and Comments

Speaking Test 2 with Responses, Analysis, and Comments

ANSWER KEYS & APPENDICES

PART 1 – LISTENING PREPARATION: MET IDIOMS

Idioms are included in the conversations and discussions that you will hear on the listening section of the MET. So, knowledge of idioms is essential for success on your exam. Get ready to ace your listening test by studying the idioms in this section. Then try the listening practice tests in the next section of the study guide.

Instructions: In the list below, the definition of each idiom or expression is followed by the idiom in a sentence. You should study the grammatical construction of each sentence and try to memorize each idiom, and you may want to make flashcards for this purpose. When you have finished, you should do the idiom exercises after each section.

Idioms – A to F

apply oneself - to work very hard on a specific task. e.g. - If we apply ourselves, we should be able to clean up the house in two hours.

be as hard as nails - relating to a person who is strong and determined. e.g. - He won't give up. He's as hard as nails.

be a wreck - to be in very bad physical condition, esp. from nervousness or exhaustion. e.g. - Mary is a wreck about her upcoming hospital stay.

be beside yourself - to be very nervous or upset. e.g. - I am just beside myself waiting for the results of my test.

be caught red-handed - to be discovered during the commission of criminal activities. e.g. - He was caught red-handed as he attempted to put the stolen merchandise in his pocket.

be in ruins - to be totally destroyed. e.g. - The town was in ruins after the hurricane.

beating around the bush - to avoid talking about a certain topic. e.g. - I tried to get an answer out of her, but she kept on beating around the bush.

bend over backwards - to go to your best effort to do something well. e.g. - I bent over backwards to do my best on my essay.

beyond my wildest dreams - to be better than your highest expectations. e.g. - My vacation in Rome was beyond my wildest dreams.

1

blow your chances - to lose all opportunities for success in an activity. e.g. - He blew his chances of buying a car by losing all his money gambling.

blue - relating to extreme sadness or depression. e.g. - Julie felt blue after her boyfriend left her. I've never seen her so down.

bored to tears - very bored. e.g. - The lesson was hardly interesting. In fact, I was bored to tears.

buck - dollar. e.g. - I bought this sweater for twelve bucks.

butter somebody up - to win someone's favor through flattery. e.g. - He tried to butter me up by saying how beautiful I looked today.

by leaps and bounds - with incredible or amazing speed. e.g. - The world population crisis is evident in certain countries, where the population has grown by leaps and bounds.

call for something - to make something necessary or required. e.g. - This recipe calls for white wine.

cast aspersions on somebody's character - to damage someone's reputation through rumors or gossip. e.g. - I would never cast aspersions on his character. In fact, I know that he is a very nice person.

cheat on - to be unfaithful to one's spouse or romantic partner. e.g. - Tom is filing for divorce because his wife was cheating on him.

check something out - to look at or verify something. e.g. - Check out the story in this newspaper. It's really amazing.

count me in - to want to participate in an activity. e.g. - I'll come to the party with you. Count me in.

crack somebody up - to amuse someone. e.g. - Terry's funny jokes really crack me up.

cross that bridge when we come to - to wait and see what happens before making a decision. e.g. - I think I might fail my exam, but I'll have to cross that bridge when I come to it.

crushed - to be very disappointed. e.g. - She was crushed when her boyfriend left her.

cut off your nose to spite your face - to hurt oneself by seeking revenge on others. e.g. - I know that you don't like your teacher, but telling her that she's stupid was cutting off your nose to spite your face.

defeat the purpose of something - to make something pointless. e.g. - If you eat cake after you exercise, it kind of defeats the purpose of working out.

dig up - to discover as a result of searching extensively. e.g. - Joe searched through his closet, trying to dig up something to wear.

don't rain on my parade - don't discourage me. e.g. - I just know I'm going to win the lottery, so don't rain on my parade!

draw the line at something - to set a limit that states what you are unwilling or unable to do. e.g. - I can help you move those boxes, but I draw the line at lifting the furniture.

drive a hard bargain - to be difficult to negotiate with. e.g. - He's not going to change his mind. He drives a hard bargain.

drop a hint - to give someone subtle ideas about something in order to express one's likes or dislikes. e.g. - He dropped a hint that he would like a new tie for his birthday.

drop in - to visit someone's home without having arranged a specific time. e.g. - You can just drop in and see me sometime.

fall into / fall into by accident - to start doing something by chance. e.g. - I hadn't planned on becoming a chef. I just fell into it by accident.

face the music - to accept reality. e.g. - Face the music! Your girlfriend isn't coming back to you.

fair-weather friend - loyal only during times of good fortune. e.g. - Don't trust him. He's a fair-weather friend.

feel together - to feel organized and well. e.g. - I wouldn't approach your boss for a raise today. She can't be feeling too together after staying out so late last night.

fizzle out - to reduce gradually in amount or quality. e.g. - Interest in our exercise class has fizzled out. There are only two students left.

flat broke - to be completely out of money. e.g. - Alan is flat broke and is considering filing for bankruptcy.

flirt with disaster - to become involved in a dangerous or risky situation. e.g. - Every time you drive over the speed limit, you are just flirting with disaster.

flog a dead horse - to speak so much about a particular topic that others become bored or fed up. e.g. - She is flogging a dead horse by continuing to complain about it. The situation won't change anyway.

for all intents and purposes - for all practical purposes; in effect. e.g. - My computer is useless for all intents and purposes since I cannot install any new software on it.

for keeps - to take possession or ownership of something forever. e.g. - He gave me a diamond ring for keeps.

Idiom Exercises – A to F

Instructions: Put the missing word or words in the idioms in each of the sentences below.

1. I didn't plan on becoming the president of the Parent-Teacher Organization. I just fell _____ .

2. She bent _____ trying to please him, but he still wasn't happy.

3. I don't mind walking for exercise, but I draw _____ at jogging.

4. He thought his child wouldn't survive the accident, and he was just _____ himself.

5. Those compliments were completely insincere. She is just trying to _____ you up.

6. That birthday party was fantastic. In fact, it was beyond my _____ .

7. You will _____ the purpose of dieting if you overeat afterwards.

8. I was bored _____ in that lecture.

9. You are _____ horse if you continue bringing that topic up. She has told you many times not to talk about it anymore.

10. He _____ his chances of getting into college by failing that exam.

get along like cats and dogs - to be entirely incompatible. e.g. - I can't live with my sister. We get along like cats and dogs.

get in touch - to get in contact with someone. e.g. - Get in touch with me next week to discuss the plan.

get on somebody's good side - to win someone's favor. e.g. - He tried to get on the teacher's good side by bringing her gifts.

get the lowdown on something - to obtain secret or inside information about something. e.g. - Did you get the lowdown? I heard a rumor that the factory is going to close.

give somebody a lift - to give someone a ride in your car. e.g. - Can you give me a lift into town?

give somebody the creeps - to frighten someone. e.g. - Horror movies give me the creeps.

give somebody a break - to stop giving harsh treatment to an individual. e.g. - What do you mean? You won't help me! Give me a break!

give somebody the benefit of the doubt - to decide to believe someone, even if you are not sure that they are telling the truth. e.g. - She said she had nothing to do with the missing money, so we gave her the benefit of the doubt.

go ballistic - to become extremely angry. e.g. - Her dad is going to go ballistic when he realizes that she snuck out last night without permission.

grab a bite - to go for a meal, esp. quickly. e.g. - Let's grab a bite for lunch.

grasping at straws - to try many alternative solutions in desperation. e.g. - You don't know the answer to the homework, so now you're grasping at straws.

grow on - to like something more than previously. e.g. - I didn't like my new school too much at first, but it has started to grow on me.

handle something - to endure or tolerate something. e.g. - I just can't handle waking up so early in the morning.

happy-go-lucky - carefree. e.g. - He's so happy-go-lucky that you'd think he didn't have a care in the world.

have a one-track mind - to have only one thing on your mind. e.g. - Paula has a one-track mind. All she ever thinks about is money.

have second thoughts - to doubt a decision you have already made or to re-think it. e.g. - I am having second thoughts about having sold my car.

heard it through the grapevine - to hear some people talking or gossiping about a subject. e.g. - I wasn't told the news about the situation directly. I heard it through the grapevine.

hit the nail on the head - to make an appropriate remark or statement. e.g. - The politician hit the nail on the head when he said that more financial aid should be offered to students.

hit the roof - to become furious. e.g. - My dad hit the roof when he found out I failed the exam.

hit the spot - to be exactly what was needed or desired. e.g. - Lemonade really hits the spot on a hot summer day.

hold a grudge - to bear resentment towards another person. e.g. - Julie is still holding a grudge because I criticized her work.

hold your tongue - to keep one's opinions to oneself. e.g. - I wanted to tell Mary off, but I held my tongue.

holding the bag - to be forced to take an action or make a decision. e.g. - Joe didn't help me as he promised and left me holding the bag.

hole yourself up - to hide away, especially in an effort to get something done. e.g. - He has holed himself up in the conference room in order to finish the report.

hop in - get inside my car. e.g. - I'll take you to the store. Hop in.

How come? - Why? e.g. - She's not going out tonight. How come?

If and only if – to indicate that a certain condition is sufficient. e.g. - I will retake the exam if and only if it is necessary.

in the red - to have a negative numerical balance. e.g. - The company had to close down after operating in the red for months.

It doesn't hold water - it's not believable. e.g. - I don't believe him. His story doesn't hold water.

It's low on my list – It's not a priority for me. e.g. - I am so busy working that cleaning the house is low on my list.

It goes without saying - it is obvious. e.g. - It goes without saying that you should know how to swim if you enter the pool.

It was a hit - it was very popular or a huge success. e.g. - The rock group's new song was a hit.

It was a piece of cake - it was very easy. e.g. - The exam was a piece of cake. I'm sure I passed.

It was a walk in the park - it was very easy. e.g. - That fitness class is a walk in the park. It's far too easy for me.

It wouldn't be the end of the world - It wouldn't be a complete disaster. e.g. - If I am not able to get this job, it wouldn't be the end of the world. I'll just apply for another one.

Instructions: Put the missing word or words in the idioms in each of the sentences below.

1.   He tried to get on her _____ by telling her compliments.

2.   My car broke down. Can you give me _____ ?

3.   It goes _____ that you need to wear warm clothes in the winter.

4.   She didn't tell me the news. I heard it through _____ .

5.   I don't believe her. Her story just _____ water.

6.   He thought he would like his new car, but he is starting to have _____

        thoughts.

7.   That test was so easy. It was just a _____ park.

8.   If I don't get there on time, it wouldn't be the end _____ .

9.   She needs to study, so she has _____ up in the library.

10.   They are always arguing. They get along like _____ .

keep in touch - to stay in contact with someone through correspondence or other communication. e.g. - Although my best friend lives miles away, we still manage to keep in touch.

Keep it down! - Be quiet! e.g. - Keep it down in there! I'm trying to study.

keep somebody posted - to keep someone informed. e.g. - We expect to hear some news next week, so we'll keep you posted.

keep the lid on it - to keep something a secret. e.g. - I'll tell you a secret if you can keep the lid on it.

kick in the teeth - to treat someone badly, especially when they need help.
e.g. - Refusing to see her when she was in the hospital was a kick in the teeth.

know something by heart - to know something from memory. e.g. - I know my credit card number by heart, so I can give it to the bank if the card gets lost.

let it slip - to divulge secret information. e.g. - That was supposed to be a secret, but Mary let it slip.

let the cat out of the bag - to divulge secret information. e.g. - I told her not to tell anyone, but she let the cat out of the bag.

lighten up - to relax. e. g. - You'd better learn to lighten up or you'll have a heart attack.

like looking for a needle in a haystack - to search for something that has many possible locations. e.g. - Searching for our lost keys on the beach was like looking for a needle in a haystack.

make heads or tails of something - to attempt to understand something with difficulty. e.g. - I can't make heads or tails of this map. Do you know which road to take?

make yourself scarce - not to keep one's normal company because a situation has caused conflict. e.g. - I haven't seen Jodi in weeks. She has made herself scarce after our argument.

make the big time - to achieve the highest level of success of a project or venture. e.g. - An actor is considered to have made the big time when he or she stars in a leading role.

make the grade - to have an acceptable standard of performance. e.g. - I didn't get to play in the game because I couldn't make the grade.

mind your own business - keep your opinions to yourself in order not to interfere in someone else's private life. e.g. - Maybe I should just mind my own business, but I think your decision is a huge mistake.

mouth off - to be rude or impudent. e.g. - You should be punished for mouthing off to your parents.

nitpick - to be overly concerned with very small details. e.g. - My boss is very demanding and nit-picks the smallest details.

nitwit - an idiot; a stupid person. e.g. - If you don't know that two and two equals four, you are a bigger nitwit than I thought!

no "if's", "and's" or "but's" - no excuses will be accepted. e.g. - You will do your homework, no "if's", "and's" or "but's"!

on schedule - to be on time. e.g. - The bus is on schedule today. We should get to work on time.

once in a blue moon - something that happens very rarely. e.g. - I don't like bowling, so I do it only once in a blue moon.

out of the blue - suddenly or by surprise. e.g. - She had only been in that job two weeks, and then out of the blue, she told us she was quitting.

out of the question - something that is impossible even to consider. e.g. - Going on vacation this year is out of the question. We just don't have enough money.

overstay one's welcome - to stay longer than one is welcome; to begin to impose upon one's host. e.g. - It was obvious that we had overstayed our welcome at her house when she asked us if we could go to a hotel.

paint a clear picture - to describe something in an expressive, vivid way. e.g. - Your personal-experience essay paints a clear picture about your time living in California.

pick a fight - to encourage a physical attack by displaying a hostile attitude. e.g. - He picked a fight by saying that I was too weak to hit him.

picked clean - being empty because other individuals have already taken all of the items. e.g. - The fruit at the grocery store was picked clean because we arrived too late in the day.

pin your hopes on something - to be very hopeful that something will happen. e.g. - I wouldn't pin your hopes on being accepted into medical school. You know how tough the competition is.

pinch pennies - to be very economical with money or in spending. e.g. - He is pinching pennies because he lost his job last month.

play with fire - to become involved in a dangerous situation. e.g. - If you decide to cheat on the test, you're really playing with fire.

pricey - very expensive. e.g. - They can eat at that pricey restaurant because they have a lot of money.

pull through - to survive an accident or illness. e.g. - The doctors say that he will pull through his accident.

put yourself in my shoes - to try to understand another person's situation. e.g. - If you'd put yourself in my shoes, you would understand why I did what I had to do.

Idiom Exercises – K to Q

Instructions: Put the missing word or words in the idioms in each of the sentences below.

1. Telling him more bad news when he is already so low would just be a kick

   _____ .

2. This article is so complicated. I can't make _____ of it.

3. If you really want to understand her, you should put yourself in _____ .

4. You should know your password _____ . Writing it down in your notebook

   isn't safe.

5. We arrived too late at the store, and it was already _____ clean.

6. Going mountain climbing without safety equipment is playing _____ .

7. I'd love to go shopping with you, but I'm afraid it's out _____ .

8. He was in critical condition, but the doctors say he will pull _____ .

9. I want to know what happens, so please keep me _____.

10. She took a cut in pay at work, so she has to _____ pennies.

recover with flying colors - to recover very well after an accident or injury. e.g. - Samira is recovering with flying colors after her operation and should be out of the hospital by the weekend.

red tape - complications or paperwork involved in government procedures or bureaucracy. e.g. - Applying for a job with the government involves a lot of red tape.

resign yourself to a situation - to accept a bad situation and stop attempting to change it for the better. e.g. - Julie used to hate living with her mother-in-law, but has finally resigned herself to the situation.

ring a bell - to sound familiar. e.g. - Now that you mention it, that story does ring a bell.

rub someone the wrong way - to irritate or annoy someone. e.g. - I know she's in love with him, but he really rubs me the wrong way.

search high and low - to search for something extensively. e.g. - I've searched high and low for my car keys, but I still can't find them.

set somebody straight - to point out a mistake in another person's behavior or thinking. e.g. - I need to set you straight. The bus leaves at 3:00, not 3:30.

set the record straight - to provide someone with correct information after they have been misinformed. e.g. - I want to set the record straight. I finished the race in 3 hours, not 2 hours.

shed light on something - to help clear up or explain something. e.g. - Could you shed some light on this homework?

show somebody the ropes - to provide someone with instructions. e.g. - He showed me the ropes on my first day of work.

skeletons in your closet - to hide secrets about your past. e.g. - Anne doesn't talk a lot about her past. I wonder if she has skeletons in her closet.

size up - to make an estimation of or decision about the value or worth of something; evaluate. e.g. - The town's residents sized up the damage caused by the earthquake.

spill the beans - to divulge secret information. e.g. - She spilled the beans about all the confidential information that I had told her.

spring up - to appear quickly or unexpectedly from a source. e.g. - A leak suddenly sprang up from the water pipe.

steer clear of - to avoid. e.g. - If you steer clear of the dangerous areas when you are in New York City, you shouldn't have any problem.

something up your sleeve - to hide information about something. e.g. - Is that all you wanted to tell me or do you have something up your sleeve?

steer clear of - to try to avoid something or someone. e.g. - He is in a terrible mood today. I would steer clear of him if I were you.

stick to your guns - not changing one's mind or opinion. e.g. - He won't change his mind because he always sticks to his guns.

stood up - to have an appointment or a date broken by someone. e.g. - I was supposed to meet Sue at 10:00, but she stood me up.

stumbling block - something that prevents or hinders progress; hindrance, obstacle, or barrier. e.g. - His poor health was a stumbling block towards his performance at work.

sweet tooth - to enjoy eating sweets very much. e.g. - Susan has a sweet tooth and enjoys eating cake and candy.

Take a hike! - Go away. Leave me alone. e.g. - A strange man was bothering me in the mall, so I told him to take a hike.

take a stab at - to try to do something, even if you are unsure about it. e.g. - I don't have much experience decorating cakes, but I'll take a stab at it.

take its / their toll - to begin to affect, esp. negatively. e.g. - Missing several nights of sleep finally took its toll on him.

talk a mile a minute - to talk very quickly. e.g. - It is difficult to understand Bob. He talks a mile a minute.

That takes the cake! - That is shocking or unbelievable. e.g. - He asked to borrow money from you again. That really takes the cake!

That's the way the cookie crumbles - That's life. e.g. - I just lost ten dollars. Oh well, that's the way the cookie crumbles.

toe the line - to conform to a rigid standard of behavior. e.g. - If you want to lose ten pounds in two weeks, you will have to toe the line set by your diet plan.

touch base - to come into contact or communicate with. e.g. - I will touch base with you next week concerning the status of the contract.

touchy - overly sensitive or moody. e.g. - She is touchy and hates being criticized.

turn on a dime - to have great flexibility in motion. e.g. - This car is one of the finest machines I have ever driven. It can turn on a dime.

turn over a new leaf - to improve one's behavior; to change for the better. e.g. - The student promised to turn over a new leaf and start handing in his homework on time.

under the weather - to feel sick or generally unwell. e.g. - John feels under the weather and has been in bed for four days.

up to doing something - to be in the mood or able to do something. e.g. - I'm not up to going out tonight. Let's stay home.

wake up and smell the coffee - to accept an unpleasant situation. e.g. - He thinks he'll get his job back, but he'd better wake up and smell the coffee.

white lie - a lie that is told in order to avoid hurting someone's feelings. e.g. - She told me that she hadn't been invited to the wedding, so I told a white lie and said I wasn't invited either.

you can count on it - you can depend on it; it is certain to happen. e.g. - You can count on her coming to the party. She promised to be there.

You made your bed, and now you can lie in it. - a person must face the consequences of his or her actions. e.g. - It was his own decision to cheat on the exam. Now that he got caught, I can only say that he made his bed, and now he can lie in it.

Idiom Exercises – R to Z

Instructions: Put the missing word or words in the idioms in each of the sentences below.

1.   I have never met him, but his name rings _____ .

2.   I told her a _____ lie to avoid hurting her feelings.

3.   If you think you are going to win the lottery, you need to wake _____ .

4.   I can't stand him. He really _____ way.

5.   We searched _____ for the special edition of the book.

6.   I haven't sung this song before, but I'll take _____ at it.

7.   After failing the college entrance exam, he said, "That's the way _____."

8.   I can't understand him. He talks a _____ .

9.   She doesn't want to be scolded again, so she has promised to turn _____ .

10.   You'd better _____ of her. She doesn't want to see anyone today.

PART 2 – MET LISTENING PRACTICE TESTS

Instructions: Understanding idioms is extremely important for the MET listening test. The most common idioms and expressions for the listening test are provided in the first section of this study guide. You may like to do the idiom exercises in the previous section before completing the practice listening tests that follow.

SOUND FILE ACCESS

To access the recordings, please go to the following webpage:

https://recordings.michigan-test.com

MET Practice Listening Test 1

Part 1

In Part 1 of the test, you will hear 19 questions.

There will be short conversations between two people.

After each conversation, you will hear a question about it.

Choose the best answer from the options printed in the practice test.

On the real test, you will have to mark your answer on a separate answer sheet.

You will hear the conversations only once.

Please listen carefully.

1)   How does the man feel about getting a scholarship?
     A. He is looking forward to it.
     B. He thinks he will be lucky.
     C. He thinks it's probably unlikely.
     D. He is hopeful.

2)   How would the man feel if the woman mentions this topic again?
     A. fed up
     B. excited
     C. resigned
     D. understanding

3)   What do we know about the man's situation?
     A. He feels enthusiastic about it.
     B. He is unhappy about his new job.
     C. He has had an argument with his boss.
     D. He is going to be fired.

4)   What does the woman suggest?
     A. That the man needs to be more patient
     B. That the man's wife has misled him
     C. That the man's wife is a difficult woman
     D. That the man and his wife go away for a few days

5)   What will the man do next?
     A. Speak to the coach.
     B. Speak to his son.
     C. Speak to the teacher.
     D. He won't take the woman's advice.

6)   What does the woman suggest?
     A. That the man gets professional help for his project
     B. That they talk before seeing each other on Saturday
     C. That they go out on Saturday
     D. That the man calls her sometime soon

7)   How does the man feel about the woman's comments?
     A. He thinks that she wants him to get the job.
     B. He thinks that she has given some good advice.
     C. He thinks that she is trying to discourage him.
     D. He thinks that she doesn't want to attend the parade.

8)   What are the speakers saying about Mary?
     A. She is not being responsible about her job.
     B. She is nervous about her work situation.
     C. She is speaking badly about other people.
     D. She has been fired.

19

9) What do we know about the speakers' friend?
   A. She is overweight.
   B. She has heart disease.
   C. She has diabetes.
   D. She eats junk food occasionally.

10) How does the man feel about the concert?
    A. He detests these events.
    B. He really enjoys classical music.
    C. He is starting to like it a bit more.
    D. He finds the music relaxing.

11) What does the man want to do?
    A. He wants to find a new bank.
    B. He wants to wait to see what happens.
    C. He wants to think about other options.
    D. He wants to take his money out of the bank.

12) What happened with the manager yesterday?
    A. He had another appointment.
    B. He apologized to the man and the woman.
    C. The employees saw him standing somewhere else.
    D. He didn't come to the appointment.

13) What happened to the speakers' classmate?
    A. He bought a video game.
    B. He was in jail for stealing.
    C. He was in bed ill.
    D. He caught something in a game.

14) Which word best describes the relationship between the woman and the man?
    A. difficult
    B. jovial
    C. acrimonious
    D. friendly

15) What was the woman's reaction to the man's comment?
    A. She thought the man should be more grateful.
    B. She knew the man would find the work challenging.
    C. She didn't realize that the man misunderstood the report.
    D. She is pleasantly surprised.

16) Why does the woman mention keys?
    A. She can't find hers.
    B. She wants to use the man's.
    C. She has lost the extra set.
    D. She wants the man to use his.

17) What does the man think about his former roommate?
   A. He doesn't like being a stockbroker.
   B. He wasted his time by staying up late.
   C. He doesn't mind what people say about him.
   D. He got the good job that he deserved.

18) What are the speakers discussing?
   A. Whether or not to invite their friend to a party
   B. How funny their mutual friend is
   C. Which people attended the man's birthday party
   D. Whether or not their friend's feelings were hurt

19) How does the man react to the woman's last statement?
   A. He thinks it would be an unnecessary risk.
   B. He thinks it was a huge disaster.
   C. He thinks they should have fought the robbers.
   D. He thinks that they got seriously hurt.

MET Practice Listening Test 1 – Part 2

In this part of the test, you will hear longer conversations.

After each conversation, you will need to answer some questions about it.

Choose your answer from the answer choices provided on the practice test.

On the real test, you will have to mark your answer on a separate answer sheet.

There are 14 questions in Part 2.

You will hear the conversations only once.

You may take notes as you listen.

Please listen carefully.

SOUND FILE ACCESS

To access the recordings, please go to the following webpage:

https://recordings.michigan-test.com

20) What reason did the student give for being late to class?
    A. She has an earlier class that finishes late.
    B. She works part-time.
    C. She takes her child to the day care center.
    D. Her little girl is ill.

21) Why does the professor say this?
    A. To express disapproval about the student's tardiness
    B. To scold the student for not making an appointment
    C. To encourage the student to speak in detail
    D. To imply that he doesn't have time to talk

22) What did the professor say about another student?
    A. She has agreed to help this student.
    B. She is unhappy about the situation.
    C. She cannot attend at 2:00 because of work.
    D. She is working full-time.

23) What did the professor suggest that the student do?
    A. Make alternative child care arrangements
    B. Attend class at a different time
    C. Discuss her problem with another student
    D. Get class notes from another student

---

24) What does the man mean when he gives this response?
    A. He doesn't know the information.
    B. He has memorized them.
    C. He understands them.
    D. He has written them down.

25) According to the woman, what problem can be encountered by computer users?
    A. They create invalid messages.
    B. They include capital letters in their passwords.
    C. They forget certain characters in their passwords.
    D. They use forbidden symbols in their passwords.

26) How does the woman solve the man's problem?
    A. By giving a step-by-step explanation
    B. By telling him to read about it
    C. By describing common problems
    D. By referring the man to another department

---

27) What is the main topic of this part of the seminar?
   A. An educational strategy
   B. The variety of assessment models available
   C. Students' willingness to learn
   D. Various types of learning materials

28) What best describes what a teacher should do in the "question adjustment" strategy?
   A. Ask questions that exceed the students' level
   B. Ask mainly easy questions
   C. Ask questions at various levels of difficulty
   D. Ask each individual student a different question

29) Which learning material does the man mention?
   A. Questions
   B. Assessments
   C. Posters
   D. Reading materials

30) Which topic is most likely to be discussed next?
   A. Informal assessment
   B. Student confidence
   C. Advanced students
   D. Formal assessment

---

31) What problem does the woman have?
   A. A friend copied her essay.
   B. She doesn't have a good idea for her essay.
   C. She copied her friend's essay.
   D. She has a disagreement with her teacher.

32) What did the professor say to the woman yesterday?
   A. She needs to work with another student.
   B. He suggested that she copied from Sarah.
   C. She needs to write on a different subject.
   D. She should write the essay on a computer.

33) What advice does the man give to the woman?
   A. To speak to Sarah
   B. To make another copy of the essay
   C. To show the professor a digital copy
   D. To follow the professor's instructions

In Part 3 of the listening test, you will hear longer talks.

You may take notes as you listen.

There are 17 questions in this part of the test.

After each talk, you will need to answer some questions about it.

Choose the best answer from the options printed in the practice test.

On the real test, you will have to mark your answer on a separate answer sheet.

You will hear the talks only once.

Please listen carefully.

SOUND FILE ACCESS

To access the recordings, please go to the following webpage:

https://recordings.michigan-test.com

34) What is the speaker talking about?
   A. a new press release
   B. a problem with a new employee
   C. how to communicate with Human Resources
   D. information about a job within the company

35) Why does the speaker mention the General Manager?
   A. He is accepting applications.
   B. He is one of the top five candidates.
   C. He will be leaving the company at the end of the month.
   D. He will be joining the company at the end of the month.

36) Why does the speaker say this?
   A. To show that this condition is the only necessary one
   B. To criticize this requirement
   C. To show that she is upset about the topic
   D. To make the audience pay attention

37) What will interested employees probably do next?
   A. Speak to Shakira.
   B. Speak to the General Manager.
   C. Improve their computer skills.
   D. Fill out an application form.

---

38) What is the main idea of this talk?
   A. Construction methods for buildings around the world
   B. Aspects of the construction of the HSBC building
   C. Construction in urban areas that have limited space
   D. The negative effect of the HSBC project on the environment

39) Why does the speaker say this?
   A. To mention where the building was erected
   B. To give details about local geology
   C. To describe the employees working on the project
   D. To highlight the origins of the building components

40) Based on the talk, what can be inferred about the basement of the building?
   A. It had to be carefully planned.
   B. It was much larger than necessary.
   C. It caused the ground in the surrounding area to be soft.
   D. It brought about the collapse of the entire building.

41) What does the speaker say about the prefabricated elements of the building?
   A. Most of them were acquired locally.
   B. They caused inconvenience to many people.
   C. They helped to avert subsidence of the structure.
   D. They constituted a large part of the project.

---

42) What have American farmers realized about organic farming?
    A. It is more expensive for the farmer.
    B. It is more cost-effective for the farmer.
    C. It results in lower profits for the farmer.
    D. It is cheaper for the consumer.

43) In what way does organic farming benefit the environment?
    A. It does not use chemicals.
    B. It uses only synthetic materials.
    C. It can be used to control produce.
    D. It challenges current regulations.

44) What comment did the speaker make about the certification process?
    A. Most farmers can pass it easily.
    B. It includes a great deal of processing.
    C. It involves quite strict standards.
    D. It happens two times per year.

45) How does organic farming improve wildlife?
    A. It results in a greater variety of species.
    B. It reduces the amount of insects.
    C. It decreases livestock.
    D. It creates unconventional species.

46) What can be inferred from this talk?
    A. Organic farming will increase in the future.
    B. Regulations on farming will become stricter.
    C. Prices for organic goods are usually higher than other goods.
    D. Most consumers prefer organic goods.

---

47) What usually happens when cells divide?
    A. the abnormal growth of organs
    B. tumors begin to grow
    C. the human body is kept healthy
    D. different types of cancer

48) What is a tumor?
    A. an organ in the human body
    B. the growth of cancer on the skin
    C. one hundred different types of disease
    D. a growth from abnormal cell division

49) What is the most common cause of cancer in America?
    A. poor nutrition
    B. overexposure to the sun
    C. smoking
    D. tobacco use in general

50) How does cancer compare to other diseases?
    A. It is the first leading cause of death.
    B. It is the second leading cause of death.
    C. It is declining each year compared to other diseases.
    D. It causes more deaths than other diseases.

SOUND FILE ACCESS

To access the recordings, please go to the following webpage:

https://recordings.michigan-test.com

Part 1

In Part 1 of the test, you will hear 19 questions.

There will be short conversations between two people.

After each conversation, you will hear a question about it.

Choose the best answer from the options printed in the practice test.

On the real test, you will have to mark your answer on a separate answer sheet.

You will hear the conversations only once.

Please listen carefully.

1)   What problem did the woman have?
    A. She had a disagreement with the man.
    B. She had a disagreement with her friend.
    C. She didn't want to hurt her friend's feelings.
    D. She believes that she made the wrong decision.

2)   What is the man going to do?
    A. Take a trip with his friends
    B. Ask his teacher a question
    C. Go away for the weekend
    D. Study for his exam

3)   What does the man suggest that the woman do?
    A. To be careful about cheating
    B. To consider what she says about others
    C. To apologize to her husband
    D. To stop complaining altogether

4)   What do the speakers say about their professor?
    A. They couldn't understand what he was saying.
    B. He talked about the essay for only a minute.
    C. He changed the date of the essay.
    D. He wasn't speaking clearly because he was ill.

5)   What can be inferred about the man?
    A. He didn't really feel afraid at the movie.
    B. He wants to watch scary movies more often.
    C. He doesn't really like scary movies.
    D. It had been a long time since he had last seen a scary movie.

6)   What do the speakers say about Toby?
    A. He will get his job back.
    B. He likes to drink coffee.
    C. He is unaware that his situation is serious.
    D. He got a poor job performance score.

7)   What can be inferred about the woman?
    A. She doesn't have children of her own right now.
    B. She lets her children decide things for themselves.
    C. She will try to persuade Amal to come to the party.
    D. Her children also toe the line.

8)   What word best describes the man's reaction to the accident?
    A. flustered
    B. accepting
    C. bored
    D. uncaring

9) Why does the woman want to talk to Carlos?
   A. To get business advice
   B. To get relationship advice
   C. To talk about time management
   D. To interview him for a job

10) What will the man probably do?
   A. Go on a hike with his friend.
   B. Nothing; he doesn't want to change.
   C. Wait to see what happens next.
   D. Try to get more comfortable.

11) What will the speakers do next?
   A. Leave the house.
   B. Do the dishes.
   C. Eat their meal.
   D. Do their homework.

12) Why is the woman upset?
   A. The man has lost her jacket.
   B. The man won't help her.
   C. She thinks the man questions her too much.
   D. She doesn't like the jacket.

13) How does the man feel about the exam?
   A. He doesn't want to speak about it.
   B. He thought it was only a bit difficult.
   C. He thinks there's a chance that he passed.
   D. He's worried that he failed.

14) What are the speakers discussing?
   A. Their friend's dress was beautiful.
   B. Their friend was going to return a worn dress.
   C. Their friend's cake was delicious.
   D. Their friend wore an old dress.

15) What was the concern of the female speaker?
   A. She doesn't like giving warnings.
   B. She wants to lessen the consequences.
   C. The employee is late to work.
   D. The employee is leaving his job.

16) What does the woman want to know?
   A. Whether the man will pay for a replacement
   B. Whether the man will clean the carpet
   C. Whether the man will paint the room
   D. Whether the man will apologize

17) Why does the woman mention her clients?
    A. She thinks the extension is too short.
    B. She thinks those jobs are more important.
    C. She thinks her boss isn't helpful.
    D. She thinks the deadline was unnecessary.

18) What is the man's reaction to the woman's opinion?
    A. He doesn't like the seminar either.
    B. He thinks the woman is right.
    C. He thinks the woman is childish.
    D. He thinks she should reconsider her opinion.

19) What are the expectations of the male speaker for his birthday?
    A. He thinks he will need to give more hints.
    B. He thinks the surprise has been ruined.
    C. He expects to be pleased.
    D. He is unsure about the situation.

MET Practice Listening Test 2 – Part 2

In this part of the test, you will hear longer conversations.

After each conversation, you will need to answer some questions about it.

Choose your answer from the answer choices provided on the practice test.

On the real test, you will have to mark your answer on a separate answer sheet.

There are 14 questions in Part 2.

You will hear the conversations only once.

You may take notes as you listen.

Please listen carefully.

SOUND FILE ACCESS

To access the recordings, please go to the following webpage:

https://recordings.michigan-test.com

20) What is the main idea of this discussion?
   A. The discovery of brain waves
   B. The reasons for brain dysfunction
   C. The principles of magnetism
   D. How to measure brain activity

21) How does the CAT scan work?
   A. By a radioactive substance
   B. By the movement of the brain
   C. By measuring a cross-section of the brain
   D. By using different colors

22) From the discussion, what can be inferred about PET scans?
   A. They are more or less identical to the CAT scan.
   B. They are superior to the MRI scan.
   C. Patients would probably rather forego PET scans.
   D. They are constantly in high demand.

23) What will the speakers probably talk about next?
   A. X-rays
   B. Magnetism
   C. Brain activity
   D. MRI scans

_____

24) What does the student mean when he says this?
   A. He is not responsible for the issue.
   B. He wants to correct his mistake.
   C. He wants to ask for leniency.
   D. He wants to emphasize the seriousness of his situation.

25) According to the member of staff, when do accommodation transfers normally take place?
   A. At the beginning of a semester
   B. In the middle of a semester
   C. At the end of a semester
   D. Only when there are urgent circumstances

26) Why does the student want to change his accommodation?
   A. His room does not have laptop facilities.
   B. He has had a dispute with a staff member.
   C. The accommodation is too far from the library.
   D. The residence hall is too noisy, and he cannot study there.

_____

27) What is the main idea of the seminar?
   A. The impact of nutrition on health
   B. The dangers of excessive dieting
   C. New advice about sugar consumption
   D. Nutrition for teenagers

28) What does the professor imply when he says this?
   A. Carbohydrates are good for the health.
   B. Carbohydrates result in low energy levels.
   C. Most people view carbohydrates negatively.
   D. Carbohydrates help to repair damage to the body.

29) What was mentioned about the nutritional requirements for teenagers?
   A. They may be suffering from health problems.
   B. They probably need more calories than adults.
   C. They may not be eating nutritious food.
   D. They need fewer calories than children.

30) Which one of the following statements is correct according to the discussion?
   A. Healthy nutrition is from five major food groups.
   B. Protein intake need not be restricted.
   C. Sugar consumption can cause health problems.
   D. Energy requirements don't change with a person's age.

_____

31) What problem does the woman have?
   A. She can't decide on the topic for her project.
   B. She doesn't know how to write the project.
   C. One of the group members isn't participating.
   D. She didn't understand the professor.

32) What class is the project for?
   A. Research Methods
   B. Earth Sciences
   C. Research & Statistics
   D. Research & Earth Science

33) What advice does the man give?
   A. To take up another part of the project
   B. To write the project alone
   C. To remove the troublesome group member
   D. To speak to the professor if necessary

In Part 3 of the listening test, you will hear longer talks.

You may take notes as you listen.

There are 17 questions in this part of the test.

After each talk, you will need to answer some questions about it.

Choose the best answer from the options printed in the practice test.

On the real test, you will have to mark your answer on a separate answer sheet.

You will hear the talks only once.

Please listen carefully.

SOUND FILE ACCESS

To access the recordings, please go to the following webpage:

https://recordings.michigan-test.com

34) Where is it usually best to begin a career in television?
   A. At the local level
   B. At the national level
   C. At the international level
   D. At the state level

35) According to the speaker, how is success measured?
   A. By the amount of money made
   B. By obtaining syndication
   C. By the number of viewers
   D. By being viewed nationwide

36) What is of utmost importance in order to get a job in journalism or broadcasting?
   A. What you know
   B. Who you know
   C. How much you know
   D. Academic degrees

37) What does the speaker mean when she says this?
   A. To have effect in the situation
   B. To be casual or foolish
   C. To be uninvolved in something
   D. To behave irresponsibly

_____

38) What is this talk mainly about?
   A. Recommendations for the NTSB
   B. The NTSB and Congress
   C. The background and purpose of the NTSB
   D. Advantages of the NTSB

39) What purpose does the NTSB serve regarding aircraft accidents?
   A. It decides if the accident was major.
   B. It investigates whether seat belts were used.
   C. It determines the cause of the accidents.
   D. It communicates with the Department of Transportation.

40) Which one of the following is the work of the NTSB?
   A. Issuing safety recommendations
   B. Investigating all road accidents
   C. Assessing the spending of the Department of Transportation
   D. Supporting the Department of Transportation

41) What is one benefit of the implementation of NTSB recommendations?
   A. Saving lives due to fewer fatal accidents
   B. Improving medical care quality
   C. Increasing wages due to injury and death
   D. Evaluating funding with Congress

_____

42) What is the main idea of this talk?
   A. To give the background to genetic engineering
   B. To discuss the current controversies of genetic engineering
   C. To describe the genetic engineering of plants
   D. To describe the genetic engineering of animals

43) What example does the professor give when discussing the earliest forms of genetic engineering?
   A. cereals and fruit
   B. insects
   C. the super tomato
   D. fish

44) What is the professor implying when he says this?
   A. The students should be paying special attention.
   B. This idea will be discussed in more detail later.
   C. The students should already be aware of this term.
   D. This idea will not be included on the examination.

45) What is gene splicing?
   A. Inserting DNA into a different organism
   B. Examining the DNA of an organism
   C. Removing all of the DNA from an organism
   D. Changing DNA for cold-water fish

46) How does the professor support his discussion of gene splicing?
   A. By identifying a common trend
   B. By drawing on statistical data
   C. By discussing the conclusions of a particular scientist
   D. By giving a specific example

---

47) Which question is central to the investigation of human choice?
   A. Do human beings have choices about their futures?
   B. Are human beings capable of making good decisions?
   C. Why do human beings have to choose?
   D. Are human beings united to each other?

48) What is epistemology?
   A. the study of being
   B. the study of knowledge
   C. the study of existence
   D. the study of emotion

49) What aspect of human personality is not investigated?
   A. emotional
   B. spiritual
   C. communal
   D. governmental

50) What is the fourth problem area of the philosophy of human nature?
   A. unity
   B. community
   C. personality
   D. thought

PART 3 – MET SPEAKING TEST PREPARATION

Purpose of the MET Speaking Test

The MET speaking test is designed to assess your communication skills in English. You will be interviewed by a trained examiner.

Format of the MET Speaking Test

The MET speaking test has five parts:

1. Task 1 – The student describes a picture. You need to speak for 60 seconds.

2. Task 2 – The student will talk about a familiar topic that is related to the picture. You need to speak for 60 seconds.

3. Task 3 – The student will need to give an opinion about a topic that is related to the picture. You need to speak for 60 seconds.

4. Task 4 –The student is expected to speak about a topic for 90 seconds without prompting from the examiner. The task involves giving someone advice about something or describing the advantages and disadvantages of something. The topic for this task is not related to the picture.

5. Task 5 – The student needs to speak persuasively about a different topic for 90 seconds. This will usually involve a controversial situation with various ideas that people have on how to solve a problem.

How the MET Speaking Test Is Scored

Your score will based on whether you can communicate effectively in English. The following criteria are usually considered:

- Fluency and Coherence

  The examiner will assess whether you can speak English naturally, without too many hesitations or long pauses. He or she will also assess whether your communication is clear and easy to understand.

- Lexical Resource

  This part of your score is based on your vocabulary in spoken English. You should aim not only to show that you have an advanced vocabulary level, but also use the vocabulary correctly in your spoken English.

- Grammatical Range and Accuracy

  The examiner will assess whether you can use a range of grammatical structures correctly in your spoken English. Accordingly, using a variety of verb tenses appropriately in your interview will help you to improve your score.

- Pronunciation

  The interviewer will consider how easy it is to understand what you are saying.

How to Prepare for the MET Speaking Test

1. **Plan ahead.** This book provides sample topics like you might face on the actual MET speaking test. Read through the topics and make notes of the kinds of phrases and responses that you might use for a given topic.

2. **Learn useful phrases for speaking.** You should study the useful phrases provided for each part of the two sample tests that follow. Please also see Appendix 2 entitled "More Useful Phrases for the Speaking Test" later in this book.

3. **Practice at home.** After you have thought about each of the topics and studied the useful phrases, you should choose a topic and practice speaking about it in front of a mirror. You should not use notes, but try to speak as freely and fluently as possible. Use a watch and keep track of the time for each part. However, don't memorize responses. Your examiner will give you a lower score if your response sounds like you have memorized it.

4. **Time yourself**. All of the speaking tasks are either sixty or ninety minutes in length. Practice speaking for sixty and ninety minutes at a time at home on a single subject. You will need to talk for the entire length of each task until the examiner stops you.

5. **Practice speaking English with friends.** This will help your spoken English to sound more natural and fluent.

6. **Improve your grammar.** Remember that your examiner will be assessing your grammar and sentence construction.

7. **Improve your vocabulary.** For a high score on the MET speaking test, you will need to show that you know some advanced vocabulary and that you can use the words correctly in sentences. Please see Appendix 3 entitled "Vocabulary Usage on the Speaking Test" to learn the key vocabulary for the most common MET speaking test topics.

Tips for Better Performance on Your MET Speaking Test

1. **Be sure to answer fully and completely.** You will not be able to demonstrate your language ability if you provide only very brief responses to the tasks. For example, if task 3 asks who you prefer to live with, you should not just respond "some friends". Instead, you should respond with complete sentences, such as: "Well, at the moment, I am living with a couple of friends. One of my roommates is a good friend that I have known since childhood, and the other one is a new friend that I met here while studying on the English foundation course". Notice how the response includes various verb tenses and sentence structures:

   - I am living – present continuous

   - is – present simple

   - I have known – present perfect

   - met – past simple

   - while studying – present participle phrase

   Responding fully in this way demonstrates that you have confidence and a good command of the English language.

2. **Don't worry about your native accent.** Some students get overly concerned about having a slight accent from their native language when speaking in English. Nevertheless, nearly all non-native speakers of English will speak with an accent. Your accent would only really cause problems if it were so strong that your examiner could not understand you. Remember that the most important thing is to speak clearly and to be understood. If you make a mistake in pronunciation when speaking, don't get flustered. Just correct yourself if you can and continue speaking.

3. **Remember that adjectives can be powerful.** Using simple one-syllable adjectives is very basic and boring. For instance, responding "My friends are nice" is something that a student with one year of English can say. It is much more powerful to use advanced adjectives, such as: "My friends are very responsible and supportive, but they can also be a little bit impetuous, which keeps our friendship exciting."

4. **Speak loudly enough.** Students sometimes think that it is better to speak in a quiet tone during the speaking test in order to show respect to the examiner. Yet, in an exam situation, this type of tone can create the impression that a student is timid or lacks confidence. It will also be difficult for the examiner if he or she has to struggle in order to hear you.

5. **Watch your speed.** Don't speak too slowly. Your speed should be like a native speaker of English.

6. **Be careful about using words from your native language.** Sometimes students "freeze" on the speaking test because they are thinking of a word in their native language and cannot remember the equivalent word in English. Don't let this happen to you. If you can't think of a word like "enrollment," just apologize and try to explain the meaning by saying something like: "Sorry, I can't remember the word, but it refers to what happens when a student begins a class at college." Then continue speaking.

Grammar and Verb Tense on Each Task of the Speaking Test

Tasks 1, 2, and 3

On tasks 1, 2 and 3 of the speaking test, you will be asked questions about familiar topics, such as your past or present activities in your current country of residence or your home country.

- **Verb tense for tasks 1 and 3**
  - When speaking for these two tasks, you should usually use the present simple, present continuous, and present perfect tenses.
  - That is because you will be talking about familiar or habitual actions, which require the present simple.
  - You may also be talking about actions that have a limited duration in the present time, which would require the present continuous.
  - On the other hand, you may be talking about activities of recent significance. In this case, the present perfect tense should be used.

- **Verb tense for task 2**
  - For task 2, you will mostly be speaking in the past tense.
  - For instance, you may be asked to talk about a person who influenced you or a favorite vacation on task 2.
  - If you are speaking about a person who influenced you or a vacation you took, you will need to use one of the past tenses since you will be describing actions or events that have taken place in the past.
  - You may have the chance to use modal verbs on tasks 1 to 3 of the speaking exam.

Tasks 4 and 5

On the fourth and fifth tasks of the speaking test, you will have to speak about different topics.

- **Conditionals and speculative language on tasks 4 and 5**

  o These topics will require you to think hypothetically and abstractly. You will also have to make generalizations and speculations.

  o Conditional sentences are useful to speculate about past and future events.

  o Using conditional sentences on these tasks will demonstrate that you have a command of advanced English grammar.

Be sure to have a look at the lists of useful phrases in each of the following sample tasks. You should try to use these or similar phrases in your responses on your MET speaking test.

We will have a look at conditional sentence structures in the following sections.

Conditional Sentence Review

Using Conditional Sentences to Improve Your Speaking Test Score

Tasks 4 and 5 of the speaking test turn to topics that are more difficult than those in tasks 1 to 3.

Therefore, in tasks 4 and 5 of the speaking test, you can demonstrate your grasp of advanced grammatical structures especially well.

Since task 5 of the speaking exam requires you to speculate, the use of conditional sentence structures is very useful on this part of the test.

If you can demonstrate a good command of how to use advanced sentence structures like conditionals, you should be able to raise your score on the speaking test.

We will look at how to use each of the conditionals in the next section of this book.

Please go to the next page, read the information on the different types of conditionals, and then try the exercises at the end of each section.

The Zero Conditional

The zero conditional is used to describe facts and generalizations.

In other words, we use the zero conditional when we want to describe a situation that always has the same outcome or result.

In zero conditional sentences, we can use the word "when" instead of the word "if" without changing the meaning of the sentence.

The zero conditional is formed with the present simple in both the "if clause" and the "main clause" of the sentence.

Also notice that the clauses of the conditional sentences can be inverted. This means that the positions of the clauses can be swapped.

Examples:

> If I go out in the rain, I take my umbrella.
>
> I take my umbrella if I go out in the rain.
>
> When I go out in the rain, I take my umbrella.
>
> I take my umbrella when I go out in the rain.

Zero conditional:

If . . . + present simple . . . , + present simple

Now try the exercises on the next page.

Zero Conditional – Exercises

Instructions: Form sentences in the zero conditional, using the words provided for each sentence. **Notice** that you may need to add some words when creating each sentence, such as articles and pronouns. The answers are provided at the end of the book.

1. if / he / not sleep / well / he / be / in a bad mood / next day

_____

2. I / take / bus / when / my car/ be / broken down

_____

3. you / look / more intelligent / if / wear / eyeglasses

_____

4. if / you / believe / everything on the internet / you / be / very foolish

_____

5. when / government / create / new laws / society / improve

_____

The First Conditional

The first conditional is used to describe events that could realistically happen in the future.

It can be used to state plans or intentions or to make predictions.

Plans: I will stay over at her house on Friday if the weather is bad.

Intentions: If I pass my exams, I will go to college.

Predictions: If the company does not monitor its budget, it will have financial problems.

The first conditional is formed with the present simple in the "if clause" and "will + the base form" in the "main clause" of the sentence.

Remember that the clauses of the conditional sentences can be inverted. This means that the positions of the clauses can be swapped.

Examples:

If I fail my test, I will attend English classes in the evening.

I will attend English classes in the evening if I fail my test.

First conditional:

If . . . + present simple . . . , + will + the base form

Comparing the Zero and First Conditionals

Remember that the zero conditional is used to describe events that happen in general every time they occur.

In contrast, the first conditional is used to describe events that will occur in a particular situation or at a particular time.

Look at the examples below.

Zero conditional:

Economic crisis occurs when inflation and unemployment increase.

First conditional:

Economic crisis will occur if inflation and unemployment increase.

Notice that the zero-conditional sentence above is describing an economic generalization, but the first-conditional sentence is making a prediction about future economic events.

Now try the exercises on the next page.

First Conditional – Exercises

Instructions: Form sentences in the first conditional using the words provided for each sentence. **Notice** that you may need to add some words when creating each sentence, such as articles and pronouns. The answers are provided at the end of the book.

1. if / he / do well / in / interview / he / get / job

_____

2. if / town council / disapprove of / new supermarket / company / not build / it

_____

3. staff / get / bonuses / if / work / more efficiently

_____

4. social problems / become / more serious / if / government / not intervene

_____

5. people / in this country / be unhappy / if / new members / congress / not / honest

_____

The Second Conditional

The second conditional is used to describe events in the present that are impossible because of present circumstances.

Example:

> If I knew my teacher's email address, I would send her a message.

The event of sending an email to the teacher is impossible at the present moment because the student does not have the email address.

The second conditional is also used to describe events in the future that are imaginary or extremely improbable.

Example:

> If I won a million dollars in the lottery, I would travel around the world in a private jet.

In the preceding sentence, it is extremely improbable that the speaker will win the lottery.

The second conditional is formed with the past simple in the "if clause" and "would + the base form" in the "main clause" of the sentence.

Like all conditional sentences, the clauses in second conditional sentences can be inverted.

Examples:

> If I knew my teacher's email address, I would send her a message.

> I would send my teacher a message if I knew her email address,

---

Second conditional:

If . . . + past simple . . . , + would + the base form

Comparing the First and Second Conditionals

Remember that the first conditional is used to describe events that could realistically happen in the future.

On the other hand, the second conditional is used to describe events that are imaginary, impossible, or extremely improbable.

Look at the examples below.

First conditional:

She will lose weight if she watches what she eats.

Second conditional:

She would lose weight if she watched what she ate.

Notice that in the first-conditional sentence, the speaker is confident that her friend will continue to control her calorie intake and lose weight.

However, in the second-conditional sentence, the speaker is saying that it is extremely unlikely that her friend will lose weight, perhaps because the speaker has reason to doubt her friend's commitment to dieting.

Now try the exercises on the next page.

Second Conditional – Exercises

Instructions: Form sentences in the second conditional using the words provided for each sentence. Notice that you may need to add some words when creating each sentence, such as articles and pronouns. The answers are provided at the end of the book.

1. if / people / be / more considerate / there / not be / so much / social unrest

   _____

2. if / university / decrease / tuition fees / enrollment / increase

   _____

3. he / be / ecstatic / if / marry / a princess

   _____

4. global warming / improve / if / people / conserve / more energy

   _____

5. more people / go on / vacation abroad / if / airlines / drop / their prices

   _____

The Third Conditional

The third conditional is used to talk about events in the past.

We use the third conditional to describe events from a retrospective perspective.

In other words, we use this sentence construction to describe how events in the past could have had different results.

The third conditional is formed with the past perfect in the "if clause" and "would have + past participle" in the "main clause" of the sentence.

Remember that the clauses of third conditional sentences can be inverted.

Examples:

> He would have passed his exam if he had studied more for it.
>
> If he had studied more for his exam, he would have passed it.

Third conditional:

If . . . + past perfect . . . , + would have + past participle

---

Now try the exercises on the next page.

Third Conditional – Exercises

Instructions: Form sentences in the third conditional using the words provided for each sentence. **Notice that you may need to add some words when creating each sentence, such as articles and pronouns. The answers are provided at the end of the book.**

1. if / medical authorities / pay more attention / epidemic / not occur

_____

2. if / his company / make more money / he / not claim / bankruptcy

_____

3. housing shortage / not exist / if / more accommodation / be available

_____

4. festivals / in my country / not become / so popular if / parents / not teach
   / children / about them

_____

5. pollution / not worsen / if / people / use / cars / less often

_____

Deciding Which Conditional to Use – Exercises

Sometimes students can't decide which conditional is the best to use in certain situations. The exercises below will help you distinguish when to use each type of conditional.

Instructions: You will see the "if clause" for each sentence below. Finish each sentence using the zero, first, second, or third conditional, as appropriate. Then identify which conditional you have used. Sample answers are provided at the end of the book.

1. If I pass my exam tomorrow . . .

_____

2. If I hadn't missed the bus yesterday . . .

_____

3. If the employee had not stolen the money . . .

_____

4. If water reaches 100 degrees . . .

_____

5. If the company truly wanted more staff . . .

_____

6. If the weather gets bad later this afternoon . . .

_____

7. If I lived on a deserted island . . .

_____

8. When human beings encounter difficulties in life . . .

_____

Now go on to the next section of the study guide, which gives samples of each of each part of the speaking test.

PART 4 – MET SPEAKING PRACTICE TESTS WITH RESPONSES

Speaking Test 1 with Responses and Comments

TASK 1 – TIPS AND SPEAKING SAMPLE

In task 1, you will be asked to describe a picture. Be sure to answer the following questions in your response:

- Where are they?

- Who are they?

- What are they doing?

TIPS

Use descriptive adjectives in your response.

You will use mainly the present tense.

However, modal verbs or other tenses can also be used.

Take a few moments to look at the picture and think about your response before you begin speaking.

You will need to talk for 60 seconds without help from the examiner.

USEFUL PHRASES

The phrases below will be useful for part 1 of the speaking test.

- There's / There are . . .

- There isn't a . . . / There aren't any . . .

- We can't see any . . .

- At the top / bottom of the picture . . .

- In the middle of the picture . . .

- On the left / right of the picture . . .

- Prepositions: next to; in front of; behind; near; on top of; under

- It looks like . . .

- It could be a . . .

- It might be a . . .

- They could be . . .

- Maybe they are . . .

- They look as if . . .

- Another aspect is . . .

- Apart from that, . . .

- . . . due to the fact that . . .

- It is a(n) beautiful / amazing / fantastic / ordinary place.

- The most noticeable aspect is that . . .

- One of the most important features is . . .

- I get the impression that . . .

- The people are happy / bored / excited / nervous / enthusiastic.

- The picture shows / expresses / points out / focuses on how . . .

- I think / believe / suppose / am sure that . . .

- It seems / appears to me that . . .

- The situation illustrated here is . . .

- The picture looks like a typical . . .

- After they finish . . .

- Later, perhaps they will . . .

Now look the sample task and response on the following pages.

TASK 1 SAMPLE

Part 1

Instructions: For this part of the test, you will describe a picture and speak about two related topics.

Task 1 (60 seconds)

Describe the picture.

SAMPLE RESPONSE

The situation illustrated here is a business meeting. The most noticeable aspect is that

the man standing appears to be the manager. He's got a piece of paper in his hand,

which might be the agenda for the meeting. Apart from that, there are four members of staff seated at the table – two males and two females. None of the staff members have brought any documents with them. I get the impression that the members of staff aren't feeling terribly enthusiastic about the meeting, due to the fact that their facial expressions make them look a bit bored. All of them have got on professional clothing. The men are wearing suits and ties, and the women have worn business suits. There aren't any other objects that you would expect to see in an office, like computers, printers, or other devices. I suppose the picture points out how mundane working in an office can be.

COMMENTS

Notice the useful phrases from the previous list, which are **highlighted**.

Also look at how the <u>present tense</u> and the *modal verbs* are used.

The situation illustrated here <u>is</u> a business meeting. **The most noticeable aspect is that** the man standing <u>appears to be</u> the manager. <u>He's got</u> a piece of paper in his hand, which *might be* the agenda for the meeting. **Apart from that**, there <u>are</u> four members of staff <u>seated</u> at the table – two males and two females. None of the staff members <u>have brought</u> any documents with them. **I get the impression that** the members of staff <u>aren't feeling</u> terribly enthusiastic about the meeting, **due to the fact that** their facial expressions make them look a bit bored. All of them <u>have got</u> on professional clothing. The men <u>are wearing</u> suits and ties, and the women <u>have worn</u> business suits. **There aren't any** other objects that you *would* expect to see in an office, like computers, printers, or other devices. **I suppose the picture points out how** mundane working in an office *can be*.

TASK 2 – TIPS AND SPEAKING SAMPLE

In task 2, you will be asked to talk about a situation or problem that you have faced.

Be sure to answer the following questions in your response:

- Who was there?

- What happened?

- When did it happen?

- Where were you?

- How did you react?

TIPS

Be sure to answer all five of the questions above.

Use a variety of past tenses in your response, such as:

- Past simple tense

- Past continuous tense

- Past perfect tense

- Past perfect continuous

Make sure that you can speak for 60 seconds on the topic.

Study the list of useful phrases below.

USEFUL PHRASES

I got accustomed to (something / doing something).

I got used to (doing something).

I used to (do something).

I felt like . . .

For example, . . .

For instance, . . .

Anyway, . . .

As I said before, . . .

As I was saying, . . .

In any event, . . .

So, . . .

The thing was . . .

TASK 2 SAMPLE

Task 2 (60 seconds)

Tell me something about a job you have had.

SAMPLE RESPONSE

Last summer, I had a job as a cashier in a supermarket in my home town. My shift was from 6:00 in the morning to 2:00 in the afternoon, so getting used to waking up early was my first challenge. Probably the most difficult thing about the job, though, was learning all of the rules and policies about handling money and dealing with customers. For example, one day when I had been standing at the register for nearly thirty minutes without a single customer, a woman came up and asked me to give her change for a ten-dollar bill. She hadn't purchased anything, but I opened the register and gave her a five and five one's. Immediately after she had left, the manager called me over to speak to me. She then reminded me that I was not allowed to open the cash drawer unless a customer had bought something. I apologized and went home and studied the employee handbook again, in order to avoid breaking any more rules in the future. In any event, it was a great job and I thoroughly enjoyed being employed there.

COMMENTS

Notice the useful phrases from the previous list, which are **highlighted**.

Also look <u>past tenses</u> and that are used.

Last summer, I <u>had</u> a job as a cashier in a supermarket in my home town. My shift <u>was</u> from 6:00 in the morning to 2:00 in the afternoon, so **getting used to** waking up early was my first challenge. Probably the most difficult thing about the job, though, <u>was</u> <u>learning</u> all of the rules and policies about handling money and dealing with customers. **For example**, one day when I <u>had been standing</u> at the register for nearly thirty minutes without a single customer, a woman <u>came up</u> and <u>asked</u> me to give her change for a ten-dollar bill. She <u>hadn't purchased</u> anything, but I <u>opened</u> the register and <u>gave</u> her a five and five one's. After she <u>had left</u>, the manager <u>called</u> me over to speak to me. She then <u>reminded</u> me that I <u>was not allowed</u> to open the cash drawer unless a customer <u>had bought</u> something. I <u>apologized</u> and <u>went</u> home and <u>studied</u> the employee handbook again, in order to avoid breaking any more rules in the future. **In any event**, it <u>was</u> a great job and I thoroughly <u>enjoyed being employed</u> there.

Also notice that the speaker has addressed all five of the essential questions.

Who was there: The speaker and her boss

When did it happen: Last summer

Where did it happen: a supermarket in the speaker's hometown

What happened: A situation with a customer

How did the speaker react: Apologized and studied the handbook

TASK 3 – TIPS AND SPEAKING SAMPLE

In task 3, you will need to give your opinion about something. Be sure to answer the following questions in your response:

- What is your preference?

- Why do you like it?

- Why do you prefer it over other options?

TIPS

State your preference clearly.

Give reasons to support your opinion.

You will be able to use a variety of tenses in this task.

Use conditional sentence structures, if possible, to demonstrate your advanced grammar skills.

Again, you need to be sure to speak for at least 60 seconds.

Study and use the phrases in the list below.

USEFUL PHRASES

In my opinion / My opinion is . . .

I guess / imagine . . .

I believe that . . .

I can't be bothered (to do something).

I enjoy it because . . .

I don't like (something / to do something).

I don't think that . . .

I think that . . .

I prefer . . .

I would consider it to be a good idea if . . .

I wouldn't want to . . .

In my opinion, . . .

My view is that . . .

Personally, . . .

The way I see it . . .

My personal opinion is that . . .

Personally, my opinion is that . . .

To be honest / In my honest opinion, . . .

I'd definitely say that . . .

I'm absolutely certain that . . .

I'm fairly confident that . . .

I'm pretty sure that . . .

I'm positive that . . .

I'm convinced that . . .

Without a doubt, . . .

As a general rule, . . .

Some people may disagree with me, but . . .

For me/ From my point of view, . . .

Frankly, . . .

I might change my mind later, but . . .

I've always thought that . . .

Personally speaking / Speaking for myself, . . .

Task 3 (60 seconds)

Some people prefer to work for a company. Others like the freedom of being self-employed and working alone. Which do you prefer? Give reasons to support your opinion.

SAMPLE RESPONSE

Some people may disagree with me, but I would really like the challenge of working for myself. I've always thought that I would love to have my own business creating and selling customized jewelry. I believe that I'd enjoy it because I am a very creative person and my mind is always bursting with design ideas for different pieces, like earrings or bracelets. Of course, there is a concern that I would lose money if the business failed. Alternatively, I just might not be able to make enough money to earn a living. That's the downside, I suppose, but I'm fairly confident that once I have finished college, I'll be able to set up my own company and be self-employed. If I do well in college, I will other get job offers – that's for sure. I say that not to boast, but because my family is very well-known in my home country. However, I wouldn't want to work for another company since my view is that you need to follow your dreams. I might change my mind later, but that's my heart's desire right now.

COMMENTS

Notice the useful phrases from the previous list, which are **highlighted**.

Notice the *conditional sentence structures*.

Some people may disagree with me, but I would really like the challenge of working for myself. **I've always thought that** I would love to have my own business creating and selling customized jewelry. **I believe that** I'd enjoy it because I am a very creative person and my mind is always bursting with design ideas for different pieces, like earrings or bracelets. Of course, there is a concern that *I would lose money if the business failed* [second conditional]. Alternatively, I just might not be able to make enough money to earn a living. That's the downside, I suppose, but **I'm fairly confident that** once I have finished college, I'll be able to set up my own company and be self-employed. *If I do well in college, I will other get job offers* [first conditional] – that's for sure. I say that not to boast, but because my family is very well-known in my home country. However, **I wouldn't want to** work for another company since my view is that you need to follow your dreams. **I might change my mind later**, but that's my heart's desire right now.

TASK 4 – TIPS AND SPEAKING SAMPLE

In task 4, you will be asked to talk about the advantages and disadvantages of a hypothetical situation. Be sure to answer the following questions in your response:

- What are the advantages?
- What are the disadvantages?
- What advice do you give?

TIPS

Discuss both the pro's and con's.

You can sum up or give advice at the end of your talk.

Use conditional sentences in your response.

Be sure to speak for the entire 90 seconds without expecting help from the examiner.

USEFUL PHRASES

Advantage / Disadvantage

Benefit / Drawback

Pro's / Con's

Positive / Negative effect

Positive / Negative consequence

Alternatively . . .

Apart from . . .

Compared to . . .

In contrast to . . .

Instead of . . .

On the contrary . . .

On the other hand . . .

Another aspect is . . .

Apart from that, . . .

The only advantage / disadvantage . . .

One of the advantages / disadvantages . . .

Some advantages / disadvantages are . . .

A possible advantage / disadvantage is . . .

A potential advantage / disadvantage is . . .

A very important advantage / disadvantage is . . .

A more important advantage / disadvantage is . . .

The main / greatest / major / overwhelming / most significant advantage . . .

The main / greatest / major / overwhelming / most significant disadvantage . . .

The advantages outweigh the disadvantages.

The disadvantages outweigh the advantages.

I would advise you (to do something).

If I were you, I would . . .

The best thing would be to . . .

Part 2

Instructions: For this part of the test, you will complete two different tasks.

Task 4 (90 seconds)

Your friend is thinking of buying a car that is five years old. She wants to do this because she hasn't got enough money for a new car. What are the advantages and disadvantages of this plan?

SAMPLE RESPONSE

My friend is quite right to consider all of the pro's and con's before making an important decision like this one. Cars are extremely expensive to buy – even used ones – and a person also has to consider the running and maintenance costs. Presumably, my friend would save money if she bought an older car. To be honest, a person can sometimes get really good deals on second-hand cars, especially compared to brand new ones. That is probably the most significant advantage of her plan. Another aspect is that if she has time to shop around, she will be able to compare different features of the cars, like engine size and gas mileage, and then be able to get what she really wants. However, an overwhelming disadvantage is that older cars are notorious for needing repairs. She might even find that the car breaks down from time to time. If that happened, she would end up spending more money getting the car repaired, instead of saving money. A very important drawback is that she could spend all of her money on the car and find that the car didn't run at all after a week or so. This happened to another friend of mine and she was furious when the dealership wouldn't refund her money. In that case, a person could lose thousands of dollars from making a bad purchase. I can't really say if the advantages outweigh the disadvantages without knowing how much she is going to spend, but if she is really committed to the idea of buying a car, I would advise her to be sure that she gets at least a twelve month guarantee from the dealership.

COMMENTS

Notice the useful phrases from the previous list, which are **highlighted**.

Notice the *conditional sentence structures*.

My friend is quite right to consider all of the **pro's and con's** before making an important decision like this one. Cars are extremely expensive to buy – even used ones – and a person also has to consider the running and maintenance costs. Presumably, *my friend would save money if she bought an older car* [second conditional]. To be honest, a person can sometimes get really good deals on second-hand cars, especially **compared to** brand new ones. That is probably **the most significant advantage** of her plan. **Another aspect is** that *if she has time to shop around, she will be able to compare different features of the cars,* [first conditional] like engine size and gas mileage, and then be able to get what she really wants. However, **an overwhelming disadvantage** is that older cars are notorious for needing repairs. She might even find that the car breaks down from time to time. *If that happened, she would end up* [second conditional] spending more money getting the car repaired, instead of saving money. **A very important drawback** is that she could spend all of her money on the car and find that the car didn't run at all after a week or so. This happened to another friend of mine and she was furious when the dealership wouldn't refund her money. In that case, a person could lose thousands of dollars from making a bad purchase. I can't really say if **the advantages outweigh the disadvantages** without knowing how much she is going to spend, but if she is really committed to the idea of buying a car, **I would advise her to** be sure that she gets at least a twelve month guarantee from the dealership.

TASK 5 – TIPS AND SPEAKING SAMPLE

In task 5, you will be asked to speculate about a situation and persuade someone to accept your point of view. Be sure to answer the following questions in your response:

- What are the possible outcomes of the proposed plan?

- Why might others disagree with the proposed plan?

- What is your plan?

- Why is your plan better than the proposed one?

TIPS

Be sure to state your point of view clearly.

Give reasons and examples to support your argument.

Sum up and suggest what should happen next.

Use conditional sentences to express facts, generalizations, and possible outcomes.

You should also use modal verbs, in addition to the useful phrases below.

USEFUL PHRASES

I am aware that you are undecided about . . .

I am convinced that . . .

It is clear that . . .

After weighing up both sides of the argument, . . .

I can see both points of view, but . . .

Although I can understand the opposite point of view, . . .

I have come to the conclusion that . . .

It could be said that . . .

It is more likely that . . .

It is possible that . . .

It might be that . . .

It seems that . . .

It seems to me that . . .

One can expect that . . .

People tend to . . .

It seems clear to me that . . .

It would seem to me that . . .

Not everyone will agree with this, but . . .

To be perfectly frank, . . .

Having given this issue due consideration, . . .

I am of the opinion that . . .

I can't help thinking that . . .

I know this is may be the minority view, but . . .

I lean towards the opinion that . . .

I think it's fair / reasonable to say . . .

I'm entirely / quite convinced that . . .

I've come the conclusion that . . .

It could / might well be that . . .

My view / position on this issue is clear / is that . . .

All things considered, . . .

Considering all the arguments . . .

To summarize my views on the matter, . . .

I would advise that . . .

I would advise against . . .

I would suggest . . .

You / We should plan to . . .

Task 5 (90 seconds)

A local town has been having problems with vandalism and damage to the town park at night. Some people are in favor of making a new law that everyone in the town must remain at home after dark, but others disagree about this. I am the city official in charge of passing new laws. Tell me what you think about this idea, and try to persuade me to agree with you.

SAMPLE RESPONSE

I understand that the town has been having issues with vandalism in the park after dark. I am aware that you are undecided about the situation, but after considering all of the arguments, I would advise against making the curfew law. To be perfectly frank, curfews are usually ineffective because if people really want to go out, they generally do so and risk the consequences. I know that not everyone will agree with this plan because some think that we all live in a law-abiding society, but I'm afraid that just isn't the case. I believe that it is more likely that if the vandals intend to vandalize something, they will do it anyway, despite the curfew being in place. If that is true, it's fair to say that only the law-abiding citizens would be inconvenienced by staying in at night, while the vandals continue damaging the city property without heeding the law. As a compromise solution, I would advise that concerned citizens form a neighborhood watch group. The interested parties could take turns patrolling the park in groups at night in order to deter the vandals. It seems to me that this solution is the best course of action because it won't cost the town anything if it is done by unpaid volunteers from the neighborhood. You should plan to call a town meeting and ask for volunteers, and I'm sure that you will get plenty of residents to sign up. I can't help thinking that, just by virtue or having more people present in the park after dark, the vandals will be deterred. All things considered, the vandalism issue will be solved and the city will save money.

COMMENTS

Notice the useful phrases from the previous list, which are **highlighted**.

Notice the *conditional sentence structures*.

I understand that the town has been having issues with vandalism in the park after dark. **I am aware that you are undecided about** the situation, but after **considering all of the arguments**, **I would advise against** making the curfew law. **To be perfectly frank**, curfews are usually ineffective because *if people really want to go out, they generally do so* [zero conditional] and risk the consequences. I know that **not everyone will agree with this** plan because some think that we all live in a law-abiding society, but I'm afraid that just isn't the case. I believe that **it is more likely that** *if the vandals intend to vandalize something, they will do it anyway,* [first conditional] despite the curfew being in place. If that is true, **it's fair to say that** only the law-abiding citizens would be inconvenienced by staying in at night, while the vandals continue damaging the city property without heeding the law. As a compromise solution, **I would suggest that** concerned citizens form a neighborhood watch group. The interested parties could take turns patrolling the park in groups at night in order to deter the vandals. **It seems to me that** this solution is the best course of action because *it won't cost the town anything if it is done* [first conditional] by unpaid volunteers from the neighborhood. **You should plan to** call a town meeting and ask for volunteers, and I'm sure that you will get plenty of residents to sign up. **I can't help thinking that**, just by virtue or having more people present in the park after dark, the vandals will be deterred. **All things considered**, the vandalism issue will be solved and the city will save money.

TASK 1 – TIPS AND SPEAKING SAMPLE

Remember to answer the following questions in your response:

- Where are they?
- Who are they?
- What are they doing?

Also remember to use the useful phrases for each task from the previous section.

TASK 1 SAMPLE

<u>Part 1</u>

Instructions: For this part of the test, you will describe a picture and speak about two related topics.

Task 1 (60 seconds)

Describe the picture.

SAMPLE RESPONSE

This picture looks like a typical wedding. The man has got on a tuxedo, with a white shirt, bow tie, and dark shoes. The woman is wearing a white bridal gown with a shimmering train, and she has got a veil over her face. They are facing each other and holding hands. Although we can't see the woman's face very well, it looks like they both are elated to be getting married. They could be feeling a bit nervous too, since this is such a significant day for both of them. It appears to me that the man is looking at the woman with complete adoration in his eyes. They are standing in front of an archway that has been decorated with flowers and bows. Maybe they are waiting for the person who is going to perform the ceremony to arrive. We can't see any of the friends and family that probably are gathered there to celebrate with them. After they finish saying their vows, I suppose they will go to another place for a meal or dance with their loved ones.

COMMENTS

Notice the useful phrases from the list in the previous section, which are **highlighted**. Also look at how the <u>verb tenses</u> are used.

This picture looks like a typical wedding. The man <u>has got</u> on a tuxedo, with a white shirt, bow tie, and dark shoes. The woman <u>is wearing</u> a white bridal gown with a shimmering train, and she <u>has got</u> a veil over her face. They <u>are facing</u> each other and holding hands. Although **we can't see** the woman's face very well, **it looks like** they both are elated to be getting married. **They could be** feeling a bit nervous too, since this is such a significant day for both of them. **It appears to me that** the man <u>is looking</u> at the woman with complete adoration in his eyes. They <u>are standing</u> in front of an archway that <u>has been decorated</u> with flowers and bows. **Maybe they** <u>are</u> waiting for the person who is going to perform the ceremony to arrive. **We can't see** any of the friends and family that probably <u>are gathered</u> there to celebrate with them. **After they finish** saying their vows, I suppose <u>they will go</u> to another place for a meal or dance with their loved ones.

TASK 2 – TIPS AND SPEAKING SAMPLE

Remember to answer the following questions in your response:

- Who was there?

- What happened?

- When did it happen?

- Where were you?

- How did you react?

TASK 2 SAMPLE

Task 2 (60 seconds)

Tell me about something you celebrated.

SAMPLE RESPONSE

On my last birthday, my siblings threw a surprise party for me at my favorite restaurant and had invited all of my friends and relatives without me knowing anything about it. They got me to the restaurant under the ruse that my oldest sister wanted to meet a friend of hers there. Once we had arrived, my sister asked me to come with her to the restroom at the back of the restaurant, which I thought was kind of strange. Then, just before we got to the back of the restaurant, we turned off into this huge function room that I didn't even know was there. All of my friends and family had been crouching down and were hiding behind the tables, and everyone popped up and shouted "surprise" when I entered the room. Well . . . you could have knocked me over with a feather! I was so astonished that everyone had managed to get there and I knew nothing of it. I had been expecting a rather boring evening with a friend of my sister that I didn't know very well, and ended up having one of the greatest days of my life.

COMMENTS

Notice the idiom "knock me over with a feather," which is *highlighted*. This idiom means that a person is extremely surprised about something

Also look past tenses and that are used.

On my last birthday, my siblings threw a surprise party for me at my favorite restaurant and had invited all of my friends and relatives without me knowing anything about it. They got me to the restaurant under the ruse that my oldest sister wanted to meet a friend of hers there. Once we had arrived, my sister asked me to come with her to the restroom at the back of the restaurant, which I thought was kind of strange. Then, just before we got to the back of the restaurant, we turned off into this huge function room that I didn't even know was there. All of my friends and family had been crouching down and were hiding behind the tables, and everyone popped up and shouted "surprise" when I entered the room. Well . . . you could have *knocked me over with a feather*! I was so astonished that everyone had managed to get there and I knew nothing of it. I had been expecting a rather boring evening with a friend of my sister that I didn't know very well, and ended up having one of the greatest days of my life.

Also notice that the speaker has addressed all five of the essential questions.

Who was there: the speaker's friends and relatives

When did it happen: the speaker's last birthday

Where did it happen: the speaker's favorite restaurant

What happened: a surprise birthday party

How did the speaker react: she was astonished

TASK 3 – TIPS AND SPEAKING SAMPLE

Remember to answer the following questions in your response:

- What is your preference?

- Why do you like it?

- Why do you prefer it over other options?

TASK 3 SAMPLE

Task 3 (60 seconds)

Some people like to spend a lot of money to celebrate a special occasion. Others prefer to recognize these events without too much expense. How do you like to celebrate? Give reasons to support your opinion.

SAMPLE RESPONSE

I imagine that if I were a millionaire, I would spend a lot of money on every single event I wanted to celebrate. However, I'm convinced that most people aren't able to spend money in such a frivolous way. From my point of view, one can celebrate special occasions without any expense at all, by spending time with friends and family at home or by having a day out together in the park. The way I see it, having loved ones around is what makes any event memorable, rather than the amount of money that is spent. As a general rule, if a person feels loved and cherished, he or she will usually remember a special occasion with fondness. My personal opinion is that people can be rich and still feel unhappy. I'm pretty sure that most people will have heard stories in the media about cases like this. The Getty family for instance, was known as one of the wealthiest in the nation, but they had very dysfunctional family relationships. So, I'm absolutely certain that true contentment is something that no amount of money can buy.

COMMENTS

Notice the useful phrases from the list in the previous section which are **highlighted**.

Notice the *conditional sentence structures*.

I imagine that *if I were a millionaire, I would spend a lot of money* [second conditional] on every single event I wanted to celebrate. However, **I'm convinced that** most people aren't able to spend money in such a frivolous way. **From my point of view**, one can celebrate special occasions without any expense at all, by spending time with friends and family at home or by having a day out together in the park. **The way I see it,** having loved ones around is what makes any event memorable, rather than the amount of money that is spent. **As a general rule**, *if a person feels loved and cherished, he or she will usually remember* [first conditional] a special occasion with fondness. **My personal opinion is that** people can be rich and still feel unhappy. **I'm pretty sure that** most people will have heard stories in the media about cases like this. The Getty family for instance, was known as one of the wealthiest in the nation, but they had very dysfunctional family relationships. So, **I'm absolutely certain that** true contentment is something that no amount of money can buy.

TASK 4 – TIPS AND SPEAKING SAMPLE

Remember to answer the following questions in your response:

- What are the advantages?

- What are the disadvantages?

- What advice do you give?

TASK 4 SAMPLE

Part 2

Instructions: For this part of the test, you will complete two different tasks.

Task 4 (90 seconds)

The students at a private school are thinking of not attending class tomorrow in order to protest about an increase in fees. They think that doing this is the only way to stop the fees from going up. What are the advantages and disadvantages of this idea?

SAMPLE RESPONSE

The students at this school are probably thinking that the benefits of this idea outweigh the drawbacks, but I would encourage them to think carefully before they act on their plan. A potential advantage is that the school administrators will decide against the fee increase if they take note of the protest. I don't think that this is a very likely outcome, though, because school administrators can't just put their ideas into action impetuously. They have to hold meetings with the school management and the parent-teacher organization and take votes in order to decide to go ahead with their proposals. A possible drawback is that the petition could cause the students who take part in it to fall out with their parents for having been disobedient at school. However, a more important disadvantage is that there could be negative consequences for not attending classes for an entire day. A friend of mine once took part in a protest like this, and he told me that if he hadn't participated, he wouldn't have been punished by having the infraction noted on his academic record. So, if I were a student at that school, I would advise them not to go ahead with the protest. Alternatively, the best thing would be to start an online petition against the fee increase. With the power of social media, some petitions can get tens of thousands of signatures. Like the protest, the petition would get the attention of the school administrators. However, in contrast to the protest, the petition would not potentially cause harm to the academic records of any students for failure to attend classes.

COMMENTS

Notice the useful phrases from the list in the previous section, which are **highlighted**. Notice the *conditional sentence structures*.

The students at this school are probably thinking that the **benefits** of this idea outweigh the **drawbacks**, but I would encourage them to think carefully before they act on their plan. **A potential advantage is that** *the school administrators will decide against the fee increase if they take note of the protest* [first conditional]. I don't think that this is a very likely outcome, though, because school administrators can't just put their ideas into action impetuously. They have to hold meetings with the school management and the parent-teacher organization and take votes in order to decide to go ahead with their proposals. **A possible drawback** is that the petition could cause the students who take part in it to fall out with their parents for having been disobedient at school. However, **a more important disadvantage is that** there could be negative consequences for not attending classes for an entire day. A friend of mine once took part in a protest like this, and he told me that *if he hadn't participated, he wouldn't have been punished* [third conditional] by having the infraction noted on his academic record. So, *if I were a student at that school, I would advise them* [second conditional] not to go ahead with the protest. **Alternatively, the best thing would be** to start an online petition against the fee increase. With the power of social media, some petitions can get tens of thousands of signatures. Like the protest, the petition would get the attention of the school administrators. However, **in contrast to** the protest, the petition would not potentially cause harm to the academic records of any students for failure to attend classes.

TASK 5 – TIPS AND SPEAKING SAMPLE

Remember to answer the following questions in your response:

- What are the possible outcomes of the proposed plan?

- Why might others disagree with the proposed plan?

- What is your plan?

- Why is your plan better than the proposed one?

TASK 5 SAMPLE

Task 5 (90 seconds)

Your college is thinking of making all international students take a year of English classes before they can begin college, regardless of their level of English language skills. They have noticed that some students arrive at college with very poor English language skills. I am the director of the college. Tell me what you think about this idea, and try to persuade me to agree with you.

SAMPLE RESPONSE

Although I can understand the other point of view, it seems clear to me that the college's plan is rather punitive to students who have advanced levels of English language skills. While one can expect that a certain percentage of international students arriving at any college campus may have English language skills that are not up to scratch for the rigors of higher education, others may have been studying English for decades and be highly fluent in the English language. It's clear that when too many unprepared students arrive at the college, an undue burden is placed on the professors and other staff members who have to try to get the unprepared students up to speed. I lean towards the opinion, though, that some international students may have already passed English proficiency examinations, like the ECPE or the MET. There may even may be some international students who come from countries where English is widely spoken. Essentially, then, if these advanced students have to wait a year before they can begin college, they will be unduly disadvantaged. Having given this issue due consideration, I've come to the conclusion that the college should have certain exemptions in place for students who

85

can prove proficiency in English. To summarize my views on the matter, incoming students that do not have proficiency certificates should be tested and scored on a scale of English language fluency. Although some students may need a year of classes, others may be able to improve their English by taking three- or six-month courses, which the college should offer in addition to the year-long course.

COMMENTS

Notice the useful phrases from the list in the previous section, which are **highlighted**. Notice the *conditional sentence structures*.

Although I can understand the other point of view, it seems clear to me that the college's plan is rather punitive to students who have advanced levels of English language skills. While **one can expect that** a certain percentage of international students arriving at any college campus may have English language skills that are not up to scratch for the rigors of higher education, others may have been studying English for decades and be highly fluent in the English language. **It's clear that** *when too many unprepared students arrive at the college, an undue burden is placed* [zero conditional] on the professors and other staff members who have to try to get the unprepared students up to speed. **I lean towards the opinion** though, that some international students may have already passed English proficiency examinations, like the ECPE or the MET. There may even may be some international students who come from countries where English is widely spoken. Essentially, then, *if these advanced students have to wait a year before they can begin college, they will be unduly disadvantaged* [first conditional]. **Having given this issue due consideration, I've come to the conclusion that** the college should have certain exemptions in place for students who can prove proficiency in English. To summarize my views on the matter, incoming students that do not have proficiency certificates should be tested and scored on a scale of English language fluency. Although some students may need a year of classes, others may be able to improve their English by taking three- or six-month courses, which the college should offer in addition to the year-long course.

PART 5 – 10 MORE MET PRACTICE SPEAKING TESTS

MET SPEAKING PRACTICE TEST 1

Part 1

Instructions: For this part of the test, you will describe a picture and speak about two related topics.

Task 1 (60 seconds)

Describe the picture.

Task 2 (60 seconds)

Tell me about how you like to travel.

Task 3 (60 seconds)

Some people think that they should walk as much as possible. Others like the

convenience of driving their car as often as they can. Which do you think is better? Give

reasons to support your opinion.

Instructions: For this part of the test, you will complete two different tasks.

Task 4

A friend of yours is thinking about taking a full-time job, in addition to being a full-time student. He is afraid that he will have to borrow money to pay for his education. What are the advantages and disadvantages of this plan?

Task 5

The local school is thinking of discontinuing the music program to save money. Many parents disagree with this plan. I am the principal of the school. Tell me what you think about this idea, and try to persuade me to agree with you.

MET SPEAKING PRACTICE TEST 2

Part 1

Instructions: For this part of the test, you will describe a picture and speak about two related topics.

Task 1 (60 seconds)

Describe the picture.

Task 2 (60 seconds)

Tell me about a time you went out with friends.

Task 3 (60 seconds)

Some people prefer to stay in and get entertainment on their devices, while others prefer

to go out and see friends. Which do you prefer? Give reasons to support your opinion.

Instructions: For this part of the test, you will complete two different tasks.

Task 4 (90 seconds)

Your friend is thinking of quitting his job in order to travel around the world for a year. He wants to do this before he settles down and gets married. What are the advantages and disadvantages of this plan?

Task 5 (90 seconds)

The state government is thinking of passing a new law that people must be at least 25 years old before they can drive a car. They have noticed that many young adults are involved in accidents. I am a state official. Tell me what you think about this idea, and try to persuade me to agree with you.

MET SPEAKING PRACTICE TEST 3

<u>Part 1</u>

Instructions: For this part of the test, you will describe a picture and speak about two related topics.

Task 1 (60 seconds)

Describe the picture.

Task 2 (60 seconds)

Tell me about an experience you had with an animal.

Task 3 (60 seconds)

Some people like to have cats or dogs in their homes, while others think that all animals

should stay outside. Which do you think is better? Give reasons to support your opinion.

Part 2

Instructions: For this part of the test, you will complete two different tasks.

Task 4 (90 seconds)

Your friend is thinking of quitting her office job to return to college. She says that she is tired of working in an office and wants to do something else. What are the advantages and disadvantages of her plan?

Task 5 (90 seconds)

I am a company director who is thinking of making the company smaller in order to save money. To do this, three hundred people will lose their jobs. Tell me what you think about this idea, and try to persuade me to agree with you.

MET SPEAKING PRACTICE TEST 4

<u>Part 1</u>

Instructions: For this part of the test, you will describe a picture and speak about two related topics.

Task 1 (60 seconds)

Describe the picture.

Task 2 (60 seconds)

Tell me about a time you went shopping.

Task 3 (60 seconds)

Some people like to go out to shop, but others prefer to shop online. How do you like to

shop? Give reasons to support your opinion.

Instructions: For this part of the test, you will complete two different tasks.

Task 4 (90 seconds)

Your friend is thinking of trying to find work abroad. She says that she wants to do this while she is still young. What are the advantages and disadvantages of this plan?

Task 5 (90 seconds)

I am a public safety officer. I am thinking of informing the residents of my town that they cannot use cell phones while they are walking in public places. Too many people have been in accidents because of their lack of attention. Tell me what you think about this idea, and try to persuade me to agree with you.

MET SPEAKING PRACTICE TEST 5

<u>Part 1</u>

Instructions: For this part of the test, you will describe a picture and speak about two related topics.

Task 1 (60 seconds)

Describe the picture.

Task 2 (60 seconds)

Tell me about a time when you cleaned something.

Task 3 (60 seconds)

Some people like to keep their homes very clean and tidy, while others do not clean as

often. How do you like to keep your living space? Give reasons to support your opinion.

Part 2

Instructions: For this part of the test, you will complete two different tasks.

Task 4 (90 seconds)

Your friend is thinking about stopping communication with his parents. He says that they have had an argument, and he is upset. What are the advantages and disadvantages of this plan?

Task 5 (90 seconds)

The residents on a street are talking about refusing to put their trash and other waste in garbage cans, and just throwing it in the street instead. They are upset about a fee increase from the garbage collection company. I am a resident of the street. Tell me what you think about this idea, and try to persuade me to agree with you.

MET SPEAKING PRACTICE TEST 6

Part 1

Instructions: For this part of the test, you will describe a picture and speak about two related topics.

Task 1 (60 seconds)

Describe the picture.

Task 2 (60 seconds)

Tell me about a time when you worked outside.

Task 3 (60 seconds)

Some people like to spend time outdoors, while others would rather spend time indoors.

Which do you prefer? Give reasons to support your opinion.

Instructions: For this part of the test, you will complete two different tasks.

Task 4 (90 seconds)

Your friend is thinking of telling her boss that she is upset about a situation at work. She says that the situation will not change, and she needs to do something about it. What are the advantages and disadvantages of this plan?

Task 5 (90 seconds)

Your state is considering telling residents that they no longer need to get health checks from their doctors for their children before they start school. I am a health official for the state. Tell me what you think about this idea, and try to persuade me to agree with you.

<u>**Part 1**</u>

Instructions: For this part of the test, you will describe a picture and speak about two related topics.

Task 1 (60 seconds)

Describe the picture.

Task 2 (60 seconds)

Tell me about a time you cooked something.

Task 3 (60 seconds)

Some people like to cook at home, while others prefer to go out to eat. Which do you

prefer? Give reasons to support your opinion.

Instructions: For this part of the test, you will complete two different tasks.

Task 4 (90 seconds)

Your friend is thinking of starting a new business. He says that he needs to borrow $15,000 from the bank to do this. What are the advantages and disadvantages of this plan?

Task 5 (90 seconds)

Teachers at a local school are thinking about refusing to work for a month because their pay is too low. Some parents of the students at the school are upset about this, but others think it is a good idea. I am a teacher at the school. Tell me what you think about this idea, and try to persuade me to agree with you.

MET SPEAKING PRACTICE TEST 8

Part 1

Instructions: For this part of the test, you will describe a picture and speak about two related topics.

Task 1 (60 seconds)

Describe the picture.

Task 2 (60 seconds)

Tell me about a vacation you went on.

Task 3 (60 seconds)

Some people love to travel, even around the world. Others don't like crowds and prefer

to stay close to home. Which do you prefer? Give reasons to support your opinion.

Part 2

Instructions: For this part of the test, you will complete two different tasks.

Task 4 (90 seconds)

Your friend is thinking of getting a large dog that will stay in his apartment with him. He says that he feels lonely in the evenings, and he thinks the dog will be good company. What are the advantages and disadvantages of this plan?

Task 5 (90 seconds)

The number of users of a local library has fallen dramatically. Some people are in favor of closing the library to save the city money, but others disagree with this. I am the mayor in charge of the town. Tell me what you think about this idea, and try to persuade me to agree with you.

MET SPEAKING PRACTICE TEST 9

Part 1

Instructions: For this part of the test, you will describe a picture and speak about two related topics.

Task 1 (60 seconds)

Describe the picture.

Task 2 (60 seconds)

Tell me something about your hobbies.

Task 3 (60 seconds)

Some people like to participate in sports every day in order to keep in shape. Others decide to exercise less often or not to exercise at all. Which do you prefer? Give reasons to support your opinion.

Part 2

Instructions: For this part of the test, you will complete two different tasks.

Task 4 (90 seconds)

Your friend has a neighbor who is very noisy. He thinks that he should move to a different apartment to get away from the problem. What are the advantages and disadvantages of this plan?

Task 5 (90 seconds)

The local college has reported that fewer students are enrolling this year, so the bank in town is thinking of raising its fees for students who open new accounts. I am the manager of the bank. Tell me what you think about this idea, and try to persuade me to agree with you.

MET SPEAKING PRACTICE TEST 10

Part 1

Instructions: For this part of the test, you will describe a picture and speak about two related topics.

Task 1 (60 seconds)

Describe the picture.

Task 2 (60 seconds)

Tell me about a time you traveled.

Task 3 (60 seconds)

Some people like to take a lot of things with them when they travel, but others prefer to

buy what they need when they are away from home. Which do you prefer? Give reasons

to support your opinion.

Part 2

Instructions: For this part of the test, you will complete two different tasks.

Task 4 (90 seconds)

Your friend is thinking of selling all of his books before he travels abroad to study. He says that he can get a lot of money for his trip this way. What are the advantages and disadvantages of this plan?

Task 5 (90 seconds)

I am a professor at the college you are attending. The library is thinking of limiting access to the wi-fi to three hours a day per person. They say that this restriction will make the internet speed faster while users are on the system. Tell me what you think about this idea, and try to persuade me to agree with you.

IDIOM EXERCISES – ANSWERS

Idioms – A to F
1. into it / into it by accident
2. over backwards
3. the line
4. beside
5. butter
6. wildest dreams
7. defeat
8. to tears
9. flogging a dead
10. blew

Idioms G to J
1. good side
2. a lift
3. without saying
4. the grapevine
5. doesn't hold
6. second
7. walk in the
8. of the world
9. holed herself
10. cats and dogs

Idioms K to Q
1. in the teeth
2. heads or tails
3. her shoes
4. by heart
5. picked
6. with fire
7. of the question
8. through
9. posted
10. pinch

Idioms R to Z
1. a bell
2. white
3. up and smell the coffee
4. rubs me the wrong
5. high and low
6. a stab
7. the cookie crumbles
8. mile a minute
9. over a new leaf
10. steer clear

LISTENING TEST 1 – ANSWERS

Test 1 – Part 1

1. The correct answer is C. The expression "I should be so lucky" is used ironically to express that a person is unlikely to get what he or she wants.

2. The correct answer is A. The expression "I wish you'd quit flogging a dead horse" means that a topic has been discussed too much. We can also understand from the tone of the man's voice that he is fed up.

3. The correct answer is B. The man says "yes" when his female boss asks: "Is that why you asked for your old job back?" So, we can assume he is unhappy about his new job.

4. The correct answer is D. The woman suggests that "the two of you just need a weekend away to recharge and reconnect."

5. The correct answer is D. The man says "I'm not up to that" which means that he does not feel like doing what the woman suggests.

6. The correct answer is B. The woman says that on Saturday morning, they can "touch base," which means communicate with each other. The man then asks her to call him.

7. The correct answer is C. "Don't rain on my parade" means the same thing as "Don't discourage me."

8. The correct answer is A. The man suggests that Mary is lazy, and the woman says that she can't understand why Mary hasn't been fired. So, they think that Mary isn't being responsible about her job.

9. The correct answer is A. We know that the friend eats a lot of junk food. The woman also says: "There are things like diabetes and heart disease to think about at that weight." So, we can assume that the friend is overweight.

10. The correct answer is C. The expression "It's starting to grow on me" means that a person is beginning to find something more likeable or enjoyable.

11. The correct answer is B. The expression "We'll cross that bridge when we come to it" means that we should just wait and see what happens.

12. The correct answer is D. The phrase "he stood me up" means the same thing as "he didn't come."

13. The correct answer is B. The woman says that their classmate is in the county jail because "he stole a video game from the store and got caught."

14. The correct answer is C. The man and woman are angry with each other. "Acrimonious" means angry and full of bad feeling.

15. The correct answer is D. The woman responds "Oh wow," so she is pleasantly surprised.

16. The correct answer is A. The woman says: "Have you got any idea where I have left my keys?" So, we know that she can't find them right now.

17. The correct answer is D. The man agrees with the woman when she says: "I guess it really was worth all his late nights in the library studying." So, he thinks his roommate got what he deserved.

18. The correct answer is B. The speakers use the words "cracks me up," "in stitches," and "hilarious," which refer to someone who is very funny.

19. The correct answer is A. "Flirt with disaster" means to take a huge risk that will probably not have a good outcome.

Test 1 – Part 2

20. The correct answer is C. The woman says: "I have a little girl . . . she's four . . . and I have to drop her off at the day care center before class."

21. The correct answer is A. The professor says: "Your persistent tardiness . . . it's become a little disruptive."

22. The correct answer is C. The professor says: "there is a student in the same course, but that class meets at 2:00. She can't come then because she has a part-time job."

23. The correct answer is B. The professor proposes that the two students swap places: "maybe the two of you could change places. She could come to the 9:00 and you could take her place in the 2:00 session."

24. The correct answer is B. To "know something by heart" means that you have memorized it.

25. The correct answer is D. The woman says: "there are certain characters and symbols that you can't use in your password."

26. The correct answer is A. The woman explains: "You just need to press control-alt-delete, and the system will ask you to change your password."

27. The correct answer is A. They are discussing an educational strategy. Specifically, the speakers are discussing the question adjustment aspect of the student readiness model.

28. The correct answer is C. The man explains: "the teacher will ask questions at a variety of different levels of difficulty."

29. The correct answer is C. The man mentions "putting up posters in the classroom."

30. The correct answer is D. At the end of the talk, the woman says: "Now, let's move on to the area of formal assessment."

31. The correct answer is A. The man asks: "She copied from you, didn't she?" The woman responds: "Yeah, she sure did."

32. The correct answer is B. The woman says: "the professor spoke with me yesterday and accused me of copying from her."

33. The correct answer is C. The man explains: "If you can show your professor a copy of your essay, like on a disc . . . he can look at the date."

Test 1 – Part 3

34. The correct answer is D. The speaker says: "we will be accepting applications from internal applicants from our own company for the next two weeks" for the job vacancy.

35. The correct answer is C. The woman explains: "Ahmed will be leaving us at the end of this month, so that leaves the position of General Manager open."

36. The correct answer is A. The woman emphasizes the word "if" so she is explaining the aspects of the condition.

37. The correct answer is D. The speaker advises: "you can either fill out the application form online or print one out and send it to Shakira in Human Resources."

38. The correct answer is B. At the start, the speaker says that he will talk about: "the building of the Hong Kong and Shanghai Bank Corporation (HSBC) in Hong Kong."

39. The correct answer is D. The man goes on to explain that the prefabricated parts came from various countries around the world.

40. The correct answer is A. The speaker explains that "the disruption of the ground water supply had to be carefully pondered prior to construction of the HSBC headquarters. So, the basement of the building was made waterproof." The word "ponder" means to consider or plan something.

41. The correct answer is D. The speaker says: "a very significant proportion of this structure was prefabricated."

42. The correct answer is B. The speaker says that "organic farming is an incredibly cost-effective method."

43. The correct answer is A. The speaker says: "Organic farming relies on practices that do not harm the environment, and for this reason, chemicals and synthetic medicines are prohibited."

44. The correct answer is C. The speaker says: "The certification process is a stringent one and must be undertaken every year." The word "stringent" means strict.

45. The correct answer is A. The speaker explains that "organic farms are better for wildlife that those run conventionally. Scientists have discovered that organic farms contain more species of plants, birds, and insects."

46. The correct answer is C. At the beginning of the talk, the speaker says that organic food can "appeal to higher-priced markets."

47. The correct answer is C. The speaker says that "all internal organs of the body consist of cells, which normally divide to produce more cells when the body requires them. This is a natural, orderly process that keeps human beings healthy."

48. The correct answer is D. The speaker explains: "if a cell divides when it is not necessary, a large growth called a tumor can form."

49. The correct answer is B. The speaker says: "Skin cancer is the most common type of cancer for both men and women." She adds that skin cancer is from "repeated exposure to the sun." Be careful: smoking causes the largest amount of deaths, rather than the largest amount of cancer.

50. The correct answer is B. At the end of the talk, the speaker says: "Cancer is now the second leading cause of death in the United States."

LISTENING TEST 2 – ANSWERS

Test 2 – Part 1

1. The correct answer is C. The woman told a "white lie" to avoid hurting her friend's feelings.

2. The correct answer is D. The woman says: "you need to study [. . . for] your final exam."

3. The correct answer is B. The man says that the woman shouldn't "cast aspersions" on her friend's character. "To cast aspersions" means that you say harsh or critical things about someone else's behavior. So, he suggests that the woman should better consider what she says about others.

4. The correct answer is A. The man says that the professor "talks a mile a minute" and that he couldn't catch the instructions. "Catch" means understand in this context.

5. The correct answer is D. The man said that he goes to scary movies "only once in a blue moon," which means rarely. So, it had been quite some time since he had last seen a scary movie.

6. The correct answer is C. The man says that Toby needs to "wake up and smell the coffee," which means that a person needs to become aware of an unpleasant situation.

7. The correct answer is A. The woman says: "when I'm a parent." So, she doesn't have children now.

8. The correct answer is B. The man says: "that's the way the cookie crumbles," which means that an unlucky situation should just be accepted.

9. The correct answer is A. The woman says that she wants to "get some advice from Carlos" because he has a "successful business."

10. The correct answer is B. The woman says that the man "should try being a little bit nicer." He responds: "No way!"

11. The correct answer is D. The woman suggests: "let's finish our homework, then do the dishes, and then we can take off." So, they will do their homework first.

12. The correct answer is C. The woman says: "I just don't understand why you question me over little things sometimes!"

13. The correct answer is D. The man says: "No, and I'm just beside myself," which means that he is worried that he failed.

14. The correct answer is B. Their friend wore a dress, and then returned it to the store as if it hasn't been used.

15. The correct answer is C. The woman says: "If you keep coming in late to work like this, there are going to be consequences."

16. The correct answer is A. The woman complains that the carpet is ruined. She then says to the man: "I hope you'll be able to pay to replace it."

17. The correct answer is B. The woman describes the clients' jobs as urgent, while explaining that she can't finish her boss's report.

18. The correct answer is D. The man says the woman should give the seminar speaker "a second chance."

19. The correct answer is C. The woman tells the man: "I think you're going to be really happy," so he should expect to be pleased.

Test 2 – Part 2

20. The correct answer is D. The man says: "This afternoon, we'll be looking at the way the function, as well as the dysfunction, of the human brain is measured."

21. The correct answer is C. The woman says: "With the CAT scan . . . that's a cross-section."

22. The correct answer is C. The woman says that: "The PET scan works by means of an inert radioactive substance given to a patient." We can assume that the radioactive aspect of this treatment might make the patient nervous.

23. The correct answer is D. The man finishes the talk as follows: "we now have an MRI scan, which as you know works according to the principles of magnetism."

24. The correct answer is D. The man emphasizes the word "problem" so he wants to emphasize that the situation is serious.

25. The correct answer is A. The woman explains: "we usually don't consider any accommodation transfers until the beginning of a new semester."

26. The correct answer is D. The man says: "Well, it's really noisy. I can't study in my room."

27. The correct answer is A. The man begins the talk by saying: "we're going to talk about good nutrition. A healthy diet should include food from four major groups."

28. The correct answer is C. "Get bad press" means that the negative aspects of something have been in the public eye.

29. The correct answer is B. The woman says: "teenagers would probably need more calories than adults . . . because, I mean, teenagers are still in their growing phase."

30. The correct answer is C. The woman explains: "that consuming too much sugar is often connected to health problems later in life, like Type II diabetes."

31. The correct answer is C. The woman says: "one of the students in the group just isn't doing her part of the work."

32. The correct answer is A. The woman tells the man she wants to talk about the "group project for our research methods class."

33. The correct answer is D. The man advises; "If I were you, I'd give her a second chance, but if she refuses, I'd speak to the professor about it."

Test 2 – Part 3

34. The correct answer is A. The speaker says: "I'd like to begin by speaking to those of you wanting to be a news anchor person or television celebrity. Well, it's usually best to start out at the local level."

35. The correct answer is C. The speaker says: "I mean that success is measured by the number of viewers watching the program."

36. The correct answer is D. At the end of the talk, the speaker explains that "if you want to be a serious television journalist . . . you may want to study journalism or broadcasting at college since some television networks consider academic training to be a very important prerequisite to obtaining these types of jobs." Be careful: what you know or personal contacts are important for jobs as a news anchor person or television celebrity.

37. The correct answer is A. The phrase "also come into play" means that something will have an effect.

38. The correct answer is C. The speaker starts by explaining the history of the NTSB, and then goes on to talk about the work of the NTSB.

39. The correct answer is C. The speaker says: "The United States Congress charges the NTSB with determining the cause of every passenger aircraft accident in the United States."

40. The correct answer is A. The speaker explains that "the NTSB issues important recommendations, which are aimed at preventing the occurrence of future accidents."

41. The correct answer is A. At the end of the talk, the speaker says: "Many benefits accrue to society when NTSB recommendations are implemented. For example, enforcement of seat belt laws has led to a significant reduction in fatal injuries."

42. The correct answer is A. At the start of the talk, the professor says: "So, first of all, we'll go into a little bit of the background information about this topic. Then, we'll move on to consider the nuts and bolts . . . the genetic aspects of genetic engineering."

43. The correct answer is A. The professor says that "scientists have been conducting genetic engineering on plants for quite a few years now . . . things like cereals and fruit, for example."

44. The correct answer is C. The professor would normally only write new information on the board. So, he assumes the students already know it.

45. The correct answer is A. The professor explains that gene splicing is "the process whereby a small part of the DNA chain for one characteristic of one organism is cut out of the DNA chain for that organism and inserted into the DNA chain of another organism from another species." So, the DNA is placed into a different organism.

46. The correct answer is D. After explaining the process of gene splicing, the professor gives the example of the super tomato.

47. The correct answer is A. At the start of the talk, the speaker says: "The first problem area, human choice, asks whether human beings can really make decisions that can change their futures."

48. The correct answer is B. The speaker explains: "Epistemology means the study of knowledge; it should not be confused with ontology, the study of being or existence."

49. The correct answer is D. The speaker says; "The third key issue, human personality, takes a look at emotional, spiritual, and communal elements . . . rather than on government or the philosophy of the state."

50. The correct answer is A. At the end of the talk, the speaker says: "Finally, the fourth problem, the unity of the human being, explores the first three areas more fully."

Answers to Speaking Test Exercises

Zero Conditional – Answers

1. If he does not sleep well, he is in a bad mood the next day.

2. I take the bus when my car is broken down.

3. You look more intelligent if you wear eyeglasses.

4. If you believe everything on the internet, you are very foolish.

5. When the government creates new laws, society improves.

First Conditional – Answers

1. If he does well in the interview, he will get the job.

2. If the town council disapproves of the new supermarket, the company will not build it.

3. The staff will get bonuses if they work more efficiently.

4. Social problems will become more serious if the government does not intervene.

5. People in this country will be unhappy if the new members of Congress are not honest.

Second Conditional – Answers

1. If people were more considerate, there would not be so much social unrest.

2. If the university decreased tuition fees, enrollment would increase.

3. He would be ecstatic if he married a princess.

4. Global warming would improve if people conserved more energy.

5. More people would go on vacations abroad if airlines dropped their prices.

Third Conditional – Answers

1. If medical authorities had paid pay more attention, the epidemic would not have occurred.

2. If his company had made more money, he would not have claimed bankruptcy.

3. The housing shortage would not have existed if more accommodation had been available.

4. Festivals in my country would not have become so popular if parents had not taught their children about them.

5. Pollution would not have worsened if people had used their cars less often.

116

Deciding Which Conditional to Use – Answers and Explanations

1. If I pass my exam tomorrow, I will be so happy.
   The word "tomorrow" indicates that we are speaking about the future, so the first conditional is needed in this sentence

2. If I hadn't missed the bus yesterday, I would not have been late to class.
   The word "yesterday" and the use of the past perfect indicate that we need the third conditional structure.

3. If the employee had not stolen the money, she would not have lost her job.
   The use of the past perfect shows that we are speaking retrospectively about a past event, so we need the third conditional structure.

4. If water reaches 100 degrees, it boils.
   The present simple tense shows that we are talking about a scientific generalization, so we need to use the zero conditional.

5. If the company truly wanted more staff, it would hire them.
   The use of the word "truly" together with the use of the past simple tense indicates that we are speaking about an improbable event. So, we need to use the second conditional.

6. If the weather gets bad later this afternoon, I will not go for a walk.
   The phrase "later this afternoon" indicates that we are speaking about the immediate future, so the first conditional is needed in this sentence

7. If I lived on a deserted island, I would miss my family so much.
   The situation of living on a deserted island is an imaginary one for most people. Accordingly, we need to use the second conditional.

8. When human beings encounter difficulties in life, they often feel discouraged.
   The phrase "human beings" and the use of the present simple show that we are speaking about a generalization, so we need the zero conditional.

LISTENING SCRIPTS

Test 1 – Part 1

Question 1:
Will you be going to college soon?
I hope to begin in the fall.
That's great. Hopefully you'll get a full scholarship.
I should be so lucky!

Question 2:
What are your finances like right now?
I'm flat broke.
Well, I've told you before that you need to try to save a little each month.
I wish you'd quit flogging a dead horse.

Question 3:
You really take me for granted!
Oh, look . . . I'm really sorry. Wow . . . I mean, I was just hoping you'd be more enthusiastic about this. Is that why you asked for your old job back?
Yes, I just couldn't handle it anymore.
Look, I'm glad we spoke about this. I'll discuss your situation with the other managers in the meeting tomorrow.

Question 4:
My wife is really a hard woman to please.
Well, the first few months of marriage can be a bit difficult sometimes.
You're telling me!
Maybe the two of you just need a weekend away to recharge and reconnect.

Question 5:
Did your son make the varsity team?
No, he didn't make the grade.
Oh, what a shame. He's been to every practice and worked so hard. Have you considered speaking to the coach about it?
I'm not up to that.

Question 6:
Hey, Tom. Great to see you. How is your home improvement project coming along?
I thought you could shed some light on it.
Okay, I can give you a hand next time I come over. I'm free this Saturday. Can I touch base with you on Saturday morning before I leave my house?
Yes, please give me a call.

Question 7:
Have you **heard** anything yet about that new job you interviewed for?
Not yet, but I'll keep you posted.
It sounds **like** there were a lot of applicants. I know from my own experience that it can be really **hard** getting work sometimes.
Don't rain **on my** parade!

Question 8:
I wouldn't **say** she's the most industrious person I know.
I hate to **speak** badly about other people, especially Mary . . . she's done an awful lot for me . . . but . . . you know . . . she takes half hour breaks when we're only allowed ten minutes.
She's got **a lot** of nerve.
You're **right.** I don't see how she hasn't been fired yet.

Question 9:
Is your **friend still** eating a lot of junk food?
Yeah, she **eats** potato chips and candy all day long.
Um . . . To **be honest,** I'm getting a bit concerned about her health. There are things like diabetes **and heart** disease to think about at that weight.

Question 10:
Hi John. **Are you** enjoying the concert?
It's starting **to grow** on me.
When I **started** going to these events, I didn't enjoy classical music either. But I have to admit, I **do like** it now. It's so relaxing.

Question 11:
Have you **heard** the news? I've heard that they're going to close that bank **we use** on Main Street. Where are we going to put our money then?
We'll cross **that** bridge when we come to it.
Well . . . I **don't** know about that. I mean, we have some advanced warning. Maybe we should start **thinking** about our other options.

Question 12:
How did **your** appointment with the manager go yesterday?
He stood **me up.**
Oh . . . **really?** Maybe he had another appointment at the last minute or something. The same thing **happened** to me too about a month ago. He did apologize the **next** day, though.
Well, that **should** tell you something.

Question 13:
Have you **heard** that our classmate is in the county jail?
How come?
Well, he **stole** a video game from the store and got caught. Do you think **we** should go visit him **or something?**
No, he **made his** bed and now he can lie in it.

Question 14:
Come on! We need to get going. We're going to be late to the wedding.
Oh, lighten up!
Seriously?! I can't believe your attitude sometimes!
Oh, what's the point!

Question 15:
Did you have any trouble filing the report?
No, it was a piece of cake.
Oh, wow . . . I'll have to give you something more challenging next time.

Question 16:
Have you got any idea where I have left my keys?
Your guess is as good as mine.
Uh . . . Maybe I should just use the spare set.
I'll leave that up to you.

Question 17:
Is your old roommate really working in Dallas now?
Yes, he's a stockbroker there.
Wow, that's impressive. I guess it really was worth all his late nights in the library studying.
I'll say!

Question 18:
He really cracks me up.
I know. He just has everybody in stitches with his hilarious jokes. I mean, he was the heart and soul of the party when you celebrated your birthday, didn't you think so?
It was beyond my wildest dreams.
I know, right? We'll have to be sure to invite him again.

Question 19:
Were they robbed or was there a break in?
Doesn't it amount to the same thing?
Well, it probably would have been more traumatizing if they were in the store when it happened. Some victims actually try to fight back, you know.
Wow, talk about flirting with disaster.

MET Listening – Test 1, Part 2

Questions 20 to 23. *Listen to a conversation between a student and a professor.*

Student: Hi Professor Johnson. Have you got a minute?
Professor: Okay. What's up?
Student: Well, you've probably noticed that I'm usually late for your 9:00 o'clock class.
Professor: Yes, of course I have, and to be honest, I'm glad you've dropped in to talk about that. Your persistent tardiness . . . it's become a little disruptive.
Student: Well . . . I'm sorry, but it's just not going to be possible for me to be there on time. The thing is . . . I have a little girl . . . she's four . . . and I have to drop her off at the

day care center before class . . . Well . . . the day care center only opens at 9:00, so that's why I'm always late, because I have to go there first. What do you think I can do?

Professor: Look . . . there is a student in the same course, but that class meets at 2:00 o'clock. She can't come then because she has a part-time job, so if it's okay with you, maybe the two of you could change places. She could come to the 9:00 o'clock and you could take her place in the 2:00 o'clock session.

Student: Oh, yes. That would be great.

Questions 24 to 26. Listen to a conversation between two co-workers.

Speaker 1: Hi. I was wondering if you could help me.

Speaker 2: Well, let's see . . . what's your question?

Speaker 1: When I try to log in to the computer system, I keep getting an error message.

Speaker 2: Oh . . . Okay . . . Have you got your ID and password with you?

Speaker 1: No, but I know them by heart.

Speaker 2: Okay, great! Uh . . . Why don't you try to log on to this computer right here, and we'll see what happens.

Speaker 1: Okay. Here goes . . . It says something about invalid password characters.

Speaker 2: Right . . . You see, there are certain characters and symbols that you can't use in your password . . . things like the slash, the question mark, and the number sign, for example. Uh . . . You just need to press control-alt-delete, and then the system will ask you to change your password. So, then you should type in a new one that doesn't have one of those forbidden characters in it.

Questions 27 to 30. Listen to a conversation between two colleagues.

Speaker 1: Good afternoon, everyone. In our seminar today, we're going to be discussing educational strategies. So, let's look at the student readiness model. Now, who can explain the concept of "question adjustment"?

Speaker 2: Well . . . "question adjustment" means that the teacher will ask questions at a variety of different levels of difficulty. There will be some so-called "easy" questions, and then there will also be some really difficult questions, which are supposed to stretch the more capable students.

Speaker 1: Can you expand on that point? I'm thinking here about learning materials that can be used in the classroom in order to achieve "question adjustment."

Speaker 2: Are you alluding to that thing about putting up posters in the . . . uh . . . classroom with some of the questions on them, and making sure that each poster has a question of a different level of difficulty?

Speaker 1: Yes. Now, let's move on to the area of formal assessment.

Questions 31 to 33. Listen to a conversation between two friends.

Speaker 1: Hi John! Oh . . . Am I glad to see you! I'm having a problem I wanted to get your advice on.

Speaker 2: Okay. What's up?

Speaker 1: Well, I worked with Sarah in a study group for our assignment, and she asked to borrow my paper to have a look at it to get some ideas. Well, stupidly . . . because I thought I could trust her, you know . . . I let her take my essay home with her and have a look at it.

Speaker 2: Oh, no! Don't tell me what happened! She copied from you, didn't she?

Speaker 1: Yeah, she sure did. And what's worse, the professor spoke with me yesterday and accused me of copying from her! What do you think I should do?
Speaker 2: Well, if I were you, I'd speak to the professor again. The thing is, with computer files . . . they have a digital signature, showing the time and date that you last worked on them. If you can show your professor a copy of your essay, like on a disc . . . he can look at the date . . . and of course, your date will be before Sarah's, and that will show that she copied from you.
Speaker 1: That's a great idea. I'll speak with Professor Thompson again tomorrow. Thanks a lot!

MET Listening – Test 1, Part 3

Questions 34 to 37: Listen to the director of a company.

Okay everybody. Thanks for coming to this special meeting today. Could everyone have a seat please? Okay. Great. Thanks.

The reason we're meeting today is to discuss some important changes to the management structure of our company.

As some of you already know, Ahmed will be leaving us at the end of this month, so that leaves the position of General Manager open as of the first of next month.
We wanted to let you all know that we will be accepting applications from internal applicants from our own company for the next two weeks. This will be followed by interviews for the top five candidates.

If . . . and I should say here, only if . . . we are unable to fill the General Manager position with a current employee, we will then advertise the job vacancy in the press. If you are interested in applying, you can either fill out the application form online or print one out and send it to Shakira in Human Resources.

So, what are we looking for in terms of job requirements? Well, you'll need to have at least five years of managerial experience either here or at another company. You'll need to have excellent interpersonal skills and also time-management skills. And of course, it goes without saying that you'll need top notch references and proficient computer skills.

Questions 38 to 41: Listen to a presentation to an engineering class.

Skyscrapers vary around the world from city to city, depending on local climate, conditions and, of course, terrain. This is especially true in the world's most heavily populated cities. No recent construction project exemplifies this more clearly than the building of the Hong Kong and Shanghai Bank Corporation (HSBC) in Hong Kong.

First of all, it is interesting to note that a very significant proportion of this structure was prefabricated. In other words, the building was designed so that it had many pre-built parts that were not constructed on site. This prefabrication made the project a truly international effort. The windows were manufactured in Austria, the exterior walls were fabricated in the United States, the toilets and air-conditioning were made in Japan, and many of the other components came from Germany.

The HSBC building consists of 47 stories, which is an immense contrast to the twenty-story buildings in its vicinity. In fact, the previous buildings constructed on this site were limited by the soft and often waterlogged ground in the surrounding area. For this reason, the disruption of the ground water supply had to be carefully pondered prior to construction of the HSBC headquarters. So, the basement of the building was made waterproof by constructing massive concrete walls, which were built on site section-by-section.

Questions 42 to 46: *Listen to part of a radio program.*

Organic farming has become one of the fastest growing trends in agriculture recently. American farmers have realized that organic farming is an incredibly cost-effective method because it can potentially be used to control costs, as well as to appeal to higher-priced markets.

Apart from these monetary benefits, organic farming also naturally results in positive ecological outcomes for the environment. Organic farming relies on practices that do not harm the environment, and for this reason, chemicals and synthetic medicines are prohibited.

In order for agricultural products to be certified as organic, they must be grown and processed according to regulations established by the USDA, the United States Department of Agriculture. The certification process is a stringent one and must be undertaken every year.

Last but not least, organic farms are better for wildlife that those run conventionally. Scientists have discovered that organic farms contain more species of plants, birds, and insects.

Questions 47 to 50: *Listen to a professor speaking to a class.*

Cancer, a group of more than 100 different types of disease, occurs when cells in the body begin to divide abnormally. Importantly, all internal organs of the body consist of cells, which normally divide to produce more cells when the body requires them. This is a natural, orderly process that keeps human beings healthy. However, if a cell divides when it is not necessary, a large growth called a tumor can form.

Smoking is the largest single cause of death from cancer in the United States. Choice of food can also be linked to cancer. Research shows that there is a link between high-fat food and certain cancers. Skin cancer is the most common type of cancer for both men and women. Repeated exposure to the sun, through sunbathing for example, greatly increases a person's chance of developing this kind of cancer.

Cancer is now the second leading cause of death in the United States. One-third of all American women and half of all American men will develop some form of cancer during their lifetimes.

Test 2 – Part 1

Question 1:
I had to decide in that moment whether to lie to her or to tell the truth and **upset** her.
Well, I hope you chose the lesser of two evils.
I hope I did. I ended up telling her a white lie in the end. Don't you think it **was the right** thing to do?
Yeah, I agree whole-heartedly.

Question 2:
How about coming on a road trip with us this weekend?
No, I'm afraid it's out of the question.
Oh, right, you need to study. Is your final exam really that important though?
You bet! It can make the difference between passing and failing.

Question 3:
I just heard **that** she is cheating on her husband.
Well, you'd **better** not cast aspersions on her character.
No . . . I know . . . You're totally right. I gossip way too much.

Question 4:
I couldn't **make out** what the professor was saying.
I know. He **talks** a mile a minute.
Did he say **that** the essay is due on Friday?
Don't even ask! I didn't catch it.

Question 5:
Did the movie scare you?
Yeah, it gave me the creeps.
Do you go to scary movies often?
No, only once in a blue moon.

Question 6:
Toby thinks that he will get his job back, even though he insulted the boss.
Well, I think he'd better wake up and smell the coffee.
Yeah, I know. He just seems to be oblivious to the situation. I mean, how **out** of it can a person be?
Yeah, what a zero.

Question 7:
Amal told me that she can't go to the party. Her dad won't let her. He must be really strict.
Yeah, he really makes her toe the line.
Well, I just can't understand that. I mean, I think that when I'm a parent, I'll **let** my children make their own decisions when they get older.

Question 8:
I heard your car was completely wrecked in the accident. Are you upset about it?
No, that's the way the cookie crumbles.
You know what? You're right. The important thing is that no one got injured.

Question 9:
I'd really like to get some advice from Carlos. He's been running a successful business now for 25 years, you know.
Well, he must be doing something right.
Absolutely! I hope he has time to talk to me.

Question 10:
I told her to take a hike!
Oh really? Uh . . . I know it's none of my business, but maybe you should try being a little bit nicer to her.
No way! What you see is what you get!
Well, I guess you have to know what you're comfortable with.

Question 11:
Do you want to come with us?
Yeah, count me in.
Great, let's finish our homework, then do the dishes, and then we can take off.

Question 12:
I can't find my jacket anywhere.
Have you really searched high and low?
Uh . . . How frustrating . . . I just don't understand why you question me over little things like this sometimes!
Wow! What's come over you?

Question 13:
Well, what did you make of that exam?
Can I be frank?
Yeah, of course. That's why I asked. So do you think you passed?
No, and I'm just beside myself.

Question 14:
She wore that dress to the party with the tags hidden, then she returned it to the shop the next day to get her money back.
That really takes the cake!
Yeah, I know. And it's not the first time she's done it either. She's going to get caught one of these times.

Question 15:
If you keep coming in late to work like this, there are going to be consequences.
I see where you're going with this.
Yeah, that's right. Consider this your last warning.
That's good to know.

Question 16:
Who spilled this paint all over the place? The carpeting is ruined.
That's my fault, I'm afraid.
Well, I hope you'll be able to pay to replace it.
Okay, no problem at all.

Question 17:
I'm afraid I'm not going to be able to finish this report by the deadline you set.
Well, I can give you a two-week extension. Would that be helpful?
Oh, yes, thanks. That gives me time to finish urgent jobs for clients.

Question 18:
Oh . . . we have got to go to that seminar again tomorrow.
What's wrong? What you got a problem with it?
Yeah, I do . . . the speaker is just so patronizing. She treats us like we're a bunch of little kids or something. I don't think I want to go again.
Well, if I were you, I'd give her a second chance.

Question 19:
Have you told your parents what you really want for your birthday?
Well, I've dropped a few hints.
Um . . . okay . . . um . . . I don't want to spoil the surprise, but I think you're going to be really happy.
Oh, that's great news!

MET Listening – Test 2, Part 2

Questions 20 to 23: *Listen to a presentation with two speakers.*

Speaker 1: This afternoon, we'll be looking at the way the function, as well as the dysfunction, of the human brain is measured. Now, in order to measure brain activity and function, there are various types of equipment. We have traditionally used CAT and PET scans for this purpose.
Speaker 2: The PET scan works by means of an inert radioactive substance given to a patient, and this allows the doctor to observe the movement of the substance through the brain. As far as the CAT scan . . . they are like an X-ray of the brain, which is then displayed on a computer screen. The PET scan shows up as one image, and that image will have different colors. With the CAT scan . . . that's a cross-section.
Speaker 1: In addition to CAT and PET scans, we now have an MRI scan, which as you know, works according to the principles of magnetism.

Questions 24 to 26: *Listen to a conversation between a student and a staff member.*

Student: Hi, I was wondering if you could help me.
Staff: Well, I hope so . . . Have you got a question?
Student: Yeah, well, a problem is more like it!
Staff: Oh . . . That doesn't sound too good.

Student: The thing is . . . I'm living in Henderson Hall right now, but I'm wondering if it will be . . . if I could move to a different residential hall. I mean, I want to move immediately, if possible.

Staff: Um, that's kind of an unorthodox request. Not many students request to be moved in the middle of a term, and we usually don't consider any accommodation transfers until the beginning of a new semester. You have to have a really strong reason why you need to move immediately. Is there anything that makes your request to move more urgent?

Student: Well, it's really noisy. I can't study in my room. So, I am finding it extremely frustrating . . . if I want to read, or write an essay or something.

Staff: Oh, I'm sorry, but that's just such a common complaint. That's why the library is open 24 hours.

Questions 27 to 30: Listen to a discussion at a seminar.

Speaker 1: So today, we're going to talk about good nutrition. A healthy diet should include food from four major groups. These four groups are carbohydrate, fruit, vegetables, and protein. Although carbohydrates seem to have gotten bad press lately, in fact, they are an essential part of healthy nutrition. Next, I want to ask at this point, do you think that it's better to give up sugar completely in order to achieve optimal health?

Speaker 2: I don't think a person should try to forego sweets altogether. It's just that consuming too much sugar is . . . is often connected to health problems later in life, like Type II diabetes.

Speaker 1: Yes, that's right. Next, let's have a look at nutritional requirements for adults. Do you think that energy requirements . . . do you think they are higher for teenagers or adults?

Speaker 2: Isn't it true that teenagers would probably need more calories than adults? Uh . . . because, I mean, teenagers are still in their growing phase.

Questions 31 to 33: Listen to a conversation between two friends.

Speaker 1: Hi Tom! Thanks for agreeing to come over to see me. I really need your help!

Speaker 2: No problem . . . but you'll have to tell me, what on earth has happened?

Speaker 1: Well, I was telling you about that group project for our research methods class.

Speaker 2: Oh, yeah, I remember you talking about that last week. Have you got a problem with it?

Speaker 1: Yeah, I do. I mean, it's not a problem with conducting the research. It's a problem with one of my classmates in the group.

Speaker 2: What's wrong?

Speaker 1: Well, one of the students in the group just isn't doing her part of the work. Now I just don't know what to do!

Speaker 2: If I were you, I'd give her a second chance, but if she refuses, I'd speak to the professor about it. Because, otherwise the rest of you will end of having her part in the project, and she'll just get an easy grade for all of your hard work.

Questions 34 to 37: Listen to a presentation to a journalism class.

Students wishing to pursue careers in television broadcasting or journalism may have many things to consider. Today, I'd like to begin by speaking to those of you wanting to be a news anchor person or television celebrity. Well, it's usually best to start out at the local level. Many people who want to break into television do so at the beginning by approaching local networks in their state. From there, your program may be syndicated on a national level if it is successful enough. Here, by "success," I mean that success is measured by the number of viewers watching the program.

Getting that first break can be very tough, though, and I can't emphasize enough that it is really important to know the right people. Very often, jobs are obtained not because of what you know, but because of who you know. So, networking and personal connections are very important.

Now, on the other hand, if you want to be a serious television journalist, that's a slightly different matter. You may want to study journalism or broadcasting at college since some television networks consider academic training to be a very important prerequisite to obtaining these types of jobs. Of course, a whole host of personality traits will also come into play.

Questions 38 to 41: Listen to a presentation at a conference.

The National Transportation Safety Board, also known as the NTSB, was established on April 1, 1967. The NTSB was an independent body, but initially received financial and administrative support from the Department of Transportation. However, the NTSB is no longer affiliated with the Department of Transportation or any of its related agencies.

The United States Congress charges the NTSB with determining the cause of every passenger aircraft accident in the United States, as well as with investigating major accidents involving other types of transportation. As a result of its investigations, the NTSB issues important recommendations, which are aimed at preventing the occurrence of future accidents and improving passenger safety.

Many benefits accrue to society when NTSB recommendations are implemented. For example, enforcement of seat belt laws has led to a significant reduction in fatal injuries. While of course having an extremely positive effect in terms of saving lives, these laws have also indirectly improved the economy since they reduce the amount of tax dollars spent on emergency medical care for crash victims, as well as lowering the amount of lost wages due to injury or death.

Questions 42 to 46: *Listen to a professor speaking to a class.*

Okay everybody. In the lecture for today, we're going to take a look at a hotly-debated and contentious topic: genetic engineering. So, first of all, we'll go into a little bit of the background information about this topic. Then, we'll move on to consider the nuts and bolts . . . the genetic aspects of genetic engineering.

It's probably no surprise to you that scientists have been conducting genetic engineering on plants for quite a few years now . . . things like cereals and fruit, for example . . . to make plants more resistant to damage from insects and disease.
As we all know, the genetic character . . . uh . . . characteristics of any organism are present in its DNA . . . DNA . . . I don't need to write that on the board, do I? . . . So, then, in order to carry out what is known as genetic engineering, gene splicing needs to be done at first. This describes the process whereby a small part of the DNA chain for one characteristic of one organism is cut out of the DNA chain for that organism and inserted into the DNA chain of another organism from another species.

This has produced results like the super tomato. Now, the super tomato was genetically engineered by inserting some DNA from cold-water fish . . . the particular gene for resistance to cold temperatures was isolated on the DNA chain of the fish and was removed. This cold-resistant gene was then re-inserted into an ordinary tomato plant . . . and lo and behold . . . we've now got tomato plants than can grow in cold weather conditions.

Questions 47 to 50: *Listen to part of a radio program.*

The study of the philosophy of human nature is often regarded as an investigation into the meaning of life. This subject usually deals with four key problem areas: human choice, human thought, human personality, and the unity of the human being.

The first problem area, human choice, asks whether human beings can really make decisions that can change their futures. In the second problem area, human thought, epistemology is considered. Epistemology means the study of knowledge; it should not be confused with ontology, the study of being or existence.

The third key issue, human personality, takes a look at emotional, spiritual, and communal elements. Importantly, the study of the communal aspect focuses on community and communication, rather than on government or the philosophy of the state. Finally, the fourth problem, the unity of the human being, explores the first three areas more fully and asks whether there is any unifying basis for human choice, thought, and personality.

APPENDIX 1 – Accessing the Recordings

This page has information on how to access the sound files for the listening test.

To access the recordings, please go to the following webpage:

https://recordings.michigan-test.com

You will find six separate recordings on the above page, organized by each part of the practice tests.

APPENDIX 2 – More Useful Phrases for the Speaking Test

This section contains more useful phrases for the MET speaking exam. The phrases have been placed into categories, according to the functions that you will need to use on the real MET speaking test. In addition to the phrases provided in each of the sample tests, you should study the following lists and try to use these words as you respond to the sample exercises in this book.

<u>Phrases for talking about the present</u>

at present

at the moment

every day

nowadays

right now

so far

until now

<u>Phrases for collecting your thoughts</u>

Anyway, . . .

As I said before, . . .

As I was saying, . . .

In any event, . . .

So, . . .

The thing is . . .

Well . . .

What I am trying to say is that . . .

<u>Phrases for emphasizing</u>

Actually, . . .

In fact, . . .

The fact is that . . .

To be honest, . . .

. . . really . . .

<u>Phrases for explaining what you mean</u>

I mean, . . .

I mean that . . .

In other words, . . .

What I mean is . . .

<u>Phrases for giving examples</u>

For example, . . .

For instance, . . .

In particular, . . .

<u>Phrases for giving generalizations</u>

as a rule

for the most part

generally speaking

in general

in most cases

on the whole

APPENDIX 3 – Vocabulary Usage on the Speaking Test

This section contains useful words for the MET speaking exam. The words have been placed into categories, according to the subjects that have most commonly appeared on past MET examinations. You may want to study the following lists and try to use these words as you respond to the sample speaking tests in this book.

Communication

cut off communication

cut ties with

email

get in touch with

give someone a call

message

to be close

to share news with someone

Companies and Work

blue-collar job

cost-effective

diminishing returns

employee

employer

to be employed

to be self-employed

to go bankrupt

white-collar job

Culture and Society

civilization

conflict

culturally acceptable

culturally insular

culture shock

diversity

globalization

misconceptions

stereotypes

Education

certificate

coursework

curriculum

degree

diploma

educator

graduate

higher education

online degrees

private schools

qualifications

Environment

climate change

environmentally friendly

global warming

pollution

traffic jams

Family, Friends, and Colleagues

acquaintance

friend

best friend

boss

co-worker

colleague

employee

employer

fiancé

fiancée

neighbor

partner

to feel homesick

to get nostalgic

to instill (something in someone)

to miss home

to miss someone

Food and Nutrition

bitter

rancid

savory

sweet

tart

calorie intake

food groups

good nutrition

healthy diet

to be malnourished

to become overweight

to get food poisoning

to go hungry

to overeat

Free Time, Hobbies, and Leisure

bowling

camping

collecting

cooking

cycling

gardening

hiking

playing a musical instrument

to avoid getting burnt out

to be a homebody

to be an avid reader

to be an enthusiast (of an activity)

to enjoy peace and quiet

to go out to eat

to go to a football game

to keep in shape

to play (a sport)

to surf the internet

to watch a movie

Local Government, Public Safety, and

Communities

budget cuts

enforce a curfew

health checks

hold a public meeting

immunizations

local users

neighborhood watch

member of a community

pass new laws

residents

stage a demonstration or protest

Newspapers, Media, and Technology

broadcast media

journalist

landline telephone

media bias

newspaper headlines

newspaper reports

online media

printed media

sensationalism

social progress

sensationalist newspaper

technological advance

technological breakthrough

technological development

technological innovation

technological revolution

to be glued to your cell phone

to subscribe to an online newspaper

Pets

cat gym

cat or dog bed

companion animal

dog house

dog sweater

flea powder

leash

pet carrier

pet clothing

pet food

to go to the veterinarian / vet

to have tags

to pet an animal

to wear a collar

toys (for a pet)

People – Adjectives

amiable

approachable

arrogant

conservative

down-to-earth

duplicitous

hard-working

hedonistic

impulsive

inspiring

liberal

motivating

neighborly

presentable

reprehensible

repulsive

respectable

self-centered

warm-hearted

welcoming

well-mannered

Places – Phrases and Adjectives

It has a(n) + adjective atmosphere.

It is a(n) + adjective place.

bustling

calm

chaotic

charming

crowded

fascinating

lively

peaceful

picturesque

popular

touristy

Relationships - Verbs

to be on a first name basis with someone

to become friends with someone

to get acquainted with someone

to get along with someone

to start a relationship with someone

to end a relationship with someone

to get engaged to someone

to get married to someone

to marry someone

to get divorced from someone

Shopping

advertising slogan

brand loyalty

brand names

consumer

consumerism

consumer goods

credit card

feel-good factor

materialism

online shopping

outdoor marketing

product placement

return an item

uncontrolled spending

to be a spendthrift

to be careful with money

to be frugal

to be stingy

Television and Entertainment

cooking programs

flat-screen TV

download (a show or movie)

game show

newscast

paid programs

reality TV programs

remote control

reruns

sitcoms

soap opera

stream (a show or movie)

talk show

wide-screen TV

Transportation

cycling paths

bus

bus stop

cable car

cars

commuting

pedestrian

subway

taxi

taxi stand

traffic congestion

train

train station

vehicles

Travel and Tourism

the vacation of a lifetime

vacation destination

resort

hordes of tourists

souvenirs

stunning views

tourist attractions

to go on a long weekend

to go on vacation

to go out of season

to go sightseeing

to learn local customs

to travel light

Made in United States
Troutdale, OR
01/09/2024

16806256R00080